ASPECTS OF ULSTER

Aspects of Ulster

JOHN OLIVER

GREYSTONE
1994

To Stella – assayed as pure gold

First published 1994

Greystone Books Ltd., Caulside Drive,
Antrim, Northern Ireland

ISBN 1 870157 25 7

Printed by W & G Baird Ltd., Antrim

Author's Preface

I penned these essays at various times over the last ten years; and I did so simply because there was something I genuinely wished to say on each topic. Two of the longer pieces stand slightly apart because they have already been published in specialist journals – the account of years of prolonged research into Ulster-Scot family history and the analysis of the Stormont Administration (complete with footnotes supporting the many necessary references and quotations). I am advised that they may now be of interest to a wider circle of readers.

If, when all twenty essays are drawn together in this little collection, they also succeed in projecting to the wider world a many-sided picture of Ulster that is positive, outward-looking and cheerful, then that will be all to the good.

Just when the full text had been set up in print in readiness for this publication, the Ceasefire announcements of 31st August and 13th October came out, creating a new situation full of promise though still fractured by constitutional instability and crippled by uncertainty. I had to weigh up – while in the very act of proof-reading – whether or not some of the essays were still relevant and helpful.

In the end I made up my mind, in consultation with my admirable Publisher, to let all the essays stand as they were, for I believe that they may help in a small way to cast some light on our past – the good times as well as the bad, the fun as well as the grief – and on our future now so bright with hope.

October 1994   J.A.O.

Aspects and Essays

On Reading and Writing Essays   1
On the Difference between living in England and living in Ulster   5
On Telling People about Ulster   11
On Being an Instonian   17
On Being treated for a Sore Back   21
On Religious Divisions   25
On Coming to the Fair   29
*On Some Ulster-Scots and their origins in Scotland   33
On Having an English Mother-in-law   47
On Saying Good-bye to Unionism and Nationalism   51
On Painting on Vellum   57
On Magilligan   61
On a Big City with Big Ideas   67
On Playing Rugby Football   71
On Learning from Boys Clubs and other Modest Affairs   77
On Just Another Day at the Office   83
On Getting to know the Great Essayist William Haslett   89
On Managing the Grammar Schools   95
On Making Good the gaps in an Ulsterman's knowledge of
    English Literature   101
†On the Stormont Administration 1921–72   105
On Visions, Dreams and New Thinking   133

* First published in *Familia*, Ulster Genealogical Review, Vol. 2, No. 3,
1987.

† First published in *Contemporary Record*, the Journal of Contemporary
British History, Vol. 5, No. 1, 1991.

On Reading and Writing Essays

When the King of France received Michel Eyquem de Montaigne – it must have been Henri Trois as the meeting took place in 1589 just a few years before Montaigne's death and at a time when the unfortunate Monarch was beset by religious strife and incessant civil war – the King found time to tell the great Essayist that he liked his Essays. Montaigne is said to have replied at once: "In that case, Sir, you must like me because the Essays are myself." And he went on, there and then, and elsewhere, to say again and again: " I am myself the substance of my book". You would be wrong to conclude that Montaigne had therefore been indulging in one monstrous ego-trip in his huge volume of intensely personal essays. Far from it. He remained modest, humorous, – and immensely readable and entertaining; not egotistical at all.

In the unlikely event of a Monarch coming to visit me at Laundry Cottage and telling me that he or she liked these Essays of mine, I should have to reply "Then, Sir or Madam, you must like Ulster for the Essays are Ulster. I have put Ulster into every one of them, a different aspect of Ulster, a view of Ulster from the inside by a man bred, born, reared, trained and employed in the Province, a view of Ulster from the outside by a man looking at it with the eye of one who knows something of how the Province works and also something of how it appears to outsiders. And if from time to time I speak of myself, I reveal something of a man shaped by the homeland he loves."

I have chosen the essay form of writing, first of all, because it is in the long tradition of English letters. Secondly, because it lends itself to the endless turning around of a subject and viewing the same subject from countless angles. Thirdly because it is the easiest way of conveying musings, second thoughts and so on without always using references, foot notes and other impediments. Fourthly, because it can lightly embrace frequent changes of stance, mood and style. And finally because it may offer a welcome relief for you, the reader, from so many solemn, bitter writings about Northern Ireland and its terrible problems.

Hold on a moment. What is an essay? What exactly are we talking about? I always like to know the rules of the game, the limits of the medium, the parameters as people say now-a-days (when they really mean perimeters) – even if I do not always abide by them and even if I go on to break away from them when the fancy takes me.

In my search for a definition I went first to the great Lexicographer, Dr.Samuel Johnson, for I knew I should get from him a robust answer: "A loose sally of the mind. An irregular, undigested piece. Not a regular or orderly composition." The Oxford English Dictionary is more urbane: "A short composition on any particular subject". Another learned opinion suggests: "A friendly, personal, informal piece of writing about anything you like."

An attempt. A first draft. Someone wrote that he tackled his subject "by way of trial and essay". I liked that idea. Or from the O.E.D., at a deeper level: "To

1

put to the proof; to test". That in turn takes us further back in time and significance to the cognate form of the word: "Assay – the trial of metals by touch, fire etc, the determination of the quantity of metal in an ore or alloy or the fineness of coin."

Is it any wonder then that I liked the concept "Ulster By Essay" for this series of essays on one of the most sorely tried, tested, tormented and yet gifted mixed communities anywhere? "Ulster BY ESSAY," indeed, was a possible title at one stage.

Turning the subject round still further – as I am always eager to do – I recall from reading French newspapers that the French form of the word Essay – essai – can also mean a try scored at Rugby football; and that gives me the spur to look at Rugby in Ulster, one of the keenest passions of my life – and one of the most enduring. In about 1924 when I was eleven St.Jude's Elementary School in Ballynafeigh got a new Headmaster, Dan Loughrey, who introduced us right away to Rugby – a game flourishing in the Province but of course never then played at such a young age. And times were hard. Few of us could afford proper kit for the game. Mad keen to play and to do well, I turned out in a handed-down jacket with an Astrakhan collar and even tried to kick a goal in my sister Sally's pointy toed, buttoned boots. From then till now (when I make a practice of going to matches at my favourite ground, Murrayfield), Rugby has proved an abiding interest, an obsessional distraction and the best antidote I know to worry and stress.

'Revenons à nos moutons'. The Essay has a long and distinguished pedigree, if a broken one. It seems to have flourished in waves, so to speak. Our first great Essayist was without doubt Sir Francis Bacon, active in the reigns of Queen Elizabeth and James the First, although I cannot agree with those critics who label him "The Father of the English Essay." Fifty years later Abraham Cowley was at the height of his popularity and fame – and his fame was truly remarkable in his day. Then fifty years on we have Addison and Steele in "The Spectator". Fifty years later Johnson and Oliver Goldsmith. Fifty years on again and we meet Charles Lamb and – oh , so different – William Hazlitt. (Although the facts are scarce Hazlitt's father seems to have come originally as a Non-Conformist Minister from County Londonderry where Hazlitts and Hasletts abound. I reckon that Hazlitt could conceivably belong to my Londonderry family tree). Another wave of Essayists arose with Hilaire Belloc, E.V.Lucas and G.K.Chesterton at the turn of the century.

One is tempted to declare that the Essay has fallen out of favour in the last generation or two but that is hardly fair. What has happened is that the Essay now appears in many of the multitude of forms promoted by modern Press and Radio. What for instance is the Fourth Leader in The Times but an Essay? Or a wayward book review by Auberon Waugh? Or a Thought for the Day on Radio Four by that most sensitive and fluent of speakers, Father Oliver McTiernan? Or one of those brilliant contributions to the Radio Programme " From Our Own Correspondent"? Or one of Roy Hattersley's amusing Endpieces in The Guardian?

Let me take this chance to question the glib notion that Sir Francis Bacon was 'The Father of the English Essay' and indeed the whole idea that any particular genre must necessarily be descended from any one leader or Father or exemplar. Bacon, the man whom no one loved, was so intelligent, so advanced, so far ahead of his times, so subtle, so compact, so metaphysical in his writing that I find it hard to think of any known essayist who was influenced by him or who resembled him in any worthwhile way. And I am quite sure that Bacon, for his part, would have scornfully refused to recognize as a pupil or disciple any writer who claimed to be influenced by him. As Pope put it so succinctly: "If parts allure thee, think how Bacon shined, The wisest, brightest, meanest of mankind. "

In any case I don't believe that many writers consciously follow a master. Painters may do; but not writers, I think. I know in my own case that when I was writing and publishing my fictional short stories in 1990 and 1991 I stopped once or twice and asked myself: "Whom am I following here? Who has influenced me? Whose style of story-writing does my style resemble?" I could think of none. Each writer is obviously so greatly influenced by his time and his place and his experiences and the urge to tell his story that he has little leisure left to start modelling himself on any Master. Needless to say we are all of us subject to thousands of influences throughout our lives with the result that lines of descent are generally impossible to trace. But still, some similarities can be secerned. One of those that strikes me again and again is the similarity which the style and tone and above all ease of manner of Robert Lynd bear to the style and charm of Charles Lamb and Oliver Goldsmith and Abraham Cowley – a disarming way of leading you into some quite important discussion without your realizing it. It would be fanciful to imagine Robert Lynd, Fleet Street journalist, chain-smoker, cliff-hanger on every office dead-line deliberately or knowingly modelling himself on any Master. Being well taught at Inst in Belfast and having absorbed a vast body of English literature through his pores, he then displayed something of the same consummate skill in easy, beguiling writing as did Lamb, Goldsmith and Cowley.

Let us take an example: "On Not Being A Philosopher", a worthwhile dissertation on Marcus Aurelius and other learned thinkers. Here he tempts us in with these opening lines:

"Have you read Epictetus lately? "No, not lately."
"Oh, you ought to read him. Tommy's been reading
him for the first time and is fearfully excited."

To my ear, Lynd might just as well have written:

"Have you seen Eric Peters lately?" "No, not lately" "Oh, you ought to look him up. Tommy bumped into him at Ravenhill last Saturday and says he would love to have a chat with you."

I should have been just as easily cajoled into going on and taking his mind on Plato and Pliny and the value of not being a Philosopher. Robert Lynd was one of the greatest.

Once more I am eager to turn the whole subject around. In the score or so of volumes of essays which I have on my shelves every single essay is written in straight prose – as one would expect. And yet there is an exception and a formidable exception at that. One of the finest and most satisfying essays in the language is Alexander Pope's "Essay on Man", packed with wise observations as well as quotable aphorisms. And it is written entirely in rhyming couplets, using iambic pentameters throughout.

You may complain that some of my Essays here contain an element of narrative, a bit of story-telling diluting the main substance of comment and reflection. In the same way my published short stories contain a bit of editorialising, a bit of commenting, or the abiding values of the public service. Why not? That is how I see life. I have never thought it worth while philosophizing in the abstract because I am keen to work from the human situation around me, from the practical case, from the real world. When for example I was doing my work on "A Philosophical Study of the Pre-suppositions and Implications of the Welfare State" in 1949 and 1950 – the first such study in the world, my Tutors believed – I can tell you I was certainly not speculating idly on the existence of man. I was in a hurry to try to understand the real significance of free Orange Juice, Mother and Child Clinics, cash benefits and so on. I refuse, I have always refused, to be bound by categories or labels.

In the Pelican Book of English Essays the Editor concludes that throughout the manifold variety of English Essays there runs in one form or another a sense of moral purpose, a zeal to edify and clarify our thoughts upon a thousand different themes. I share that zeal.

To be clear, the Essays in this collection are not all rounded, balanced and complete. For that sort of treatment the reader would be better advised to turn to my "*Working At Stormont*" or my PEP work "*Ulster To-day and To-morrow*". I am treating some of these Essays rather in the sense Dr. Johnson sketched: as loose sallies of the mind. Nor are they intended as the last word on any topic. Other people may have different and better ideas or may wish to temper my enthusiasms. But I share the zeal, indeed the impatience, to convey some sense of moral purpose. And (as I begin to look ahead towards the age of ninety) that is what I wish to do in this volume, however naively, however inadequately.

On the Difference between living in England and living in Ulster

It is hard to sum up the attitude of most ordinary Ulster people towards England. There are so many levels of thinking, so many contradictions, so many paradoxes. But let me try to sort out a few of them, allowing myself for once the luxury of some sweeping generalisations.

The desire of the great majority of Ulster people to belong to Britain, to uphold the Crown and support Britain's causes in the world is undoubted; it is as spontaneous as it is genuine.

While they cleave to Britain, they do not necessarily cleave to England. There has always been a certain reserve, a slight suspicion of England and of English domination, a lack of empathy with the ruling classes from the South of England. This has been fed in recent years by bitter disappointment at the abject failure of Direct Rule to deal effectively with the I.R.A.; after having taken away in 1972 the power to deal with internal security, they have themselves let the position get worse and worse. Direct Rule Ministers have come exclusively from English constituencies and from the House of Lords, a well-meaning but dubious practice.

There are strong links with Scotland. Wales features a lot less in people's thinking.

The Ulster dialect – wrongly taken in England as a soft Irish brogue where it is in fact much more a branch of Scots enriched with dashes of the Irish – has a quality of directness, even of bluntness, that can take outsiders by surprise. Soft flattering talk is scorned in Ulster. The worst you can say of a man's reliability is to suggest that he is "a glib fella." At the level of negotiation and public rhetoric the local speech can be harsh to sensitive ears.

On the political level few ordinary people would even contemplate unity with the Irish Republic apart from out-and-out militant Republicans and committed Nationalist leaders. But there are countless contacts every day – far more than English people think – between North and South in trade, tourism, sport, cultural and church affairs, fully as many as people wish to have. There is no limit. A strong single thread of popular sentiment at present would, if tested, quite possibly point to some form of Ulster independence and self-rule in equal partnership with Britain and Eire. Whether that would be wise or practicable I shall not pursue here.

And yet in spite of everything the practical ties with England are immensely strong and are nourished in a host of ways – by Radio, Television, British Telecom, the Post Office, the London newsprints, the trade unions and so on. One of the most influential may well turn out to be the U.C.A.S. system for admission to University and the corresponding arrangements for Polytechnics and Colleges, which dominate the lives, the careers and the eventual destinies of Sixth Formers. Ulster arrangements are in fact so meshed in with the British system that it would be extremely hard ever to disentangle them. The

5

extraordinary position is now arising under which more and more Ulster boys and girls are going to University or College in England, leaving their places in Ulster to be taken by students from the Republic, who find Ulster a lot cheaper than the South.

From the outside, from England above all, Ulster looks regrettably provincial, even though, as my wife and I have confirmed from much personal experience, Ulster is much less provincial than many parts of England, Wales or Scotland. The Ulster people have themselves largely to blame for this particular misunderstanding. They have allowed themselves to develop an attitude of inferiority, almost the attitude of a subject race, where none is needed or justified. They speak of English institutions in some awe. They let English colleagues overshadow them when working together (while privately resenting English domination). And yet, Ulster people have as many or more working links say with London than have any corresponding group in Great Britain outside the Home Counties. When in Belfast you feel more in touch with Westminster, with national affairs and with prominent national figures than, for example, when in Cumbria or Lancashire. And of course Ulster people have far more live contacts with relatives in Canada, the States, Australia or New Zealand than have most English people. Travel to and from the Province is truly enormous. It is far from being isolated.

Let me concentrate now on one aspect, the over-done respect for things English and the unnecessary feeling of inferiority which could possibly be an underlying cause of Ulster stubbornness. Let us now talk *to* Ulster people about actual, day-to-day living conditions for ordinary people in the North of England compared with conditions in Ulster.

One can't blame the weather, for it is little different. England gets your weather to-morrow, so to speak, as most North British weather comes to us from the Atlantic. A family phone call warns me that a wet evening in Larne is sure to give a wet morning in Lancaster. It rains just as much in England, certainly a lot more in Cumbria. And it is a lot colder in Spring, the result of a horrible east wind that blows through most of February, March and April and, mercifully for you, seems to moderate before it reaches Bangor. A fine Spring day in Ulster, town or country, is probably as close to perfect weather as you will get anywhere. The growing season is late in Cumbria. It would be madness to plant your early potatoes on St.Patrick's Day, for instance; it is wiser to wait a good three weeks, as I have found to my bitter cost.

It is easy to settle and live amongst the native Cumbrian people in every practical sense. They are honest, they can never be suspected of giving short change; they are neighbourly and helpful; and noticeably fair-minded within their own settled situation. They have the Anglo-Saxon qualities of being terse, even taciturn, but of course also the drawback of being poor conversationalists and not exactly over burdened with a sense of humour. Stolid would describe them; and the prevailing physical characteristics bear that out, with stocky build, blond hair, often even seemingly blanched or bleached blond, and blue eyes. Local Beauty Queens seem chosen to demonstrate those features in the flesh, the ample flesh. Another strain is the pale-skinned, fern-tickled, sandy type, the Scot who must have come down over the Border with the Scottish reivers. Yet another is the black-haired, narrow-skulled type, the Pict who may have been in Cumbria even longer than the Anglo-Saxon.

The schools are nowhere nearly as good as your Ulster schools. Any Ulster parents you speak to, now living in England, north or south or even in Scotland, will roll their eyes, sigh and fervently wish they could send their children to somewhere like the Cross and Passion, Upper Sullivan, the Rainey or St.Columb's.

One personal experience may help to illustrate several of those points. It fell to me a few years ago to help some people to amalgamate two neighbouring but contrasting schools in Cumbria, jealous rivals, and to create one new combined school. The whole complex job, starting from scratch, had to be done within twenty months against a background of mutual suspicion laced with class distinction. Under the brilliant chairmanship of Spencer Crookenden the job was completed within that time, a remarkable feat of hard work, application, common sense and – it seemed to me above all – steadfast refusal to be distracted. Every meeting of our small founding group started promptly at five o'clock in the late afternoon; stuck to the Agenda; never re-opened a decision once taken; flogged no dead horses; finished on time and had everyone back at home and sitting down to a pork pie by seven-thirty. In Ulster the group would have been twice as big, for a start. Every meeting would have gone on till midnight; every decision re-opened and debated; every member would have insisted on arguing every conceivable aspect – but a better school might have emerged.

One small point in the amalgamation horrified me and at the same time educated me. In the formal legal constitution for the proposed Board of Governors we included a place – alongside the proper quota of elected members, representative members and so on – for the local landlord and benefactor by name, his heirs and successors. At first I could hardly believe my ears; the idea was so old-fashioned and undemocratic. And yet that was exactly what the local people wanted. Nothing was being forced on them. The extraordinary decision fitted easily into the local pattern. And so I voted for it.

The point is that it fitted also into the wider pattern of class and class consciousness that still pervades rural Cumbria in the 1980s and 1990s. Everyone in the neighbourhood has his place, seems content with his place and recognizes the place of everyone else, within a hierarchical framework that has survived remarkably intact over the centuries. And the very strong sense of historical continuity is seldom commented on; it is taken for granted. All this, together with the accepted position of the Church of England, has surprised me more than anything else. If someone owns his house he is assumed to vote Tory, to belong to the Church and to uphold the Vicar. I find none of this offensive. It just seems quaint.

Just like the English road system, which is antiquated and far below the standard of your Ulster road system. Roads in England carry an A classification that would scarcely merit a C in Ulster, judging purely by width, alignment, camber, surviving bottle-necks and so on. Some of even the most modern road junctions are ugly or inefficient or both, such as Levens Bridge on the A6 (where the beautiful Levens Hall has memorabilia of Wellington and Baggott) or the Hyning junction further down the A6 (where Sir Robert Peel used to live).

The English have not yet heard of your sensible arrangement of R plates for newly qualified car drivers, still less of your modern Driving Licence with the bearer's photograph, a most practical aid to everyone except the law-breaker. Nor of your law that requires every driver to immobilize his vehicle each time he leaves it. They have a long way to go yet to catch up with you in all these ways. They are better drivers, however. In England it is possible to count more often on other drivers doing the expected thing than in Ulster where they all seem to be in such a hurry to overtake (or worse still to "undertake") or to speed away first from the traffic lights. And they seem to keep their cars in better condition in England.

In a word you have better roads but worse drivers

They are also behind the times in the ordering of their Health Service and Social Services which are still in separate – dare I say, sectarian blocks, using that word in its original meaning – even after all those scandals affecting child abuse, neglect of geriatrics, mental health in the community and so on: Health in the N.H.S. and Social Services in the County Council.

No doubt the day will come when practical common sense will bring about the merging of those two sister services as you managed to do long ago in Ulster. Finance may force the change even sooner, for the present chasm between Health on the taxes and Social Services on the local rates is too fatuous to linger much longer.

Intensive work with many active local bodies throughout Cumbria over fifteen years has given my wife and me a privileged insight into some of the ways in which local care works in practice and in relation to the individual man or woman. Voluntary bodies are numerous, energetic and caring and their relations with the statutory bodies are largely free from friction or needle. The difficult conditions under which such bodies work in Ulster – a politically divided community beset by unparalleled bombing; – makes it hard to form direct comparisons but two things can safely be said. Ulster people may feel assured that they are served by a body of workers, official, voluntary or independent, at least as efficient and responsive as those in England and certainly a lot more approachable. And you may count yourselves lucky in Ulster that your voluntary and independent bodies enjoy closer and more fruitful relations with Government Departments and the decision-makers than similar bodies in, say, Cumbria could ever dream of.

Apart from all other considerations Ulster makes a model region in many ways – self-contained, easily recognized by any citizen, not overlapped by neighbouring regions, with one big capital city and a second city at the other side of the region and every home easily reached by Ulster Radio, T.V and the three Belfast daily newspapers. Those are great advantages, never to be underestimated.

It is much much harder for people in most parts of England to recognize what region they are in for any particular purpose – health, transport, gas, electricity, water, T.V. and so on – and where its boundaries run. Few people could tell you.

Although the standard of behaviour of small business firms in England is good, it would be wrong to exaggerate it. Small builders, though less talkative than in Ulster and making fewer promises, can be just as tiresome and as maddening as small builders anywhere.

One of the most attractive features of Ulster life is sadly lacking in the North of England, namely the consistently high standard of women's dress. It used to be that one noticed the splendid dressing-up only on Sundays or at weddings; but now it extends to everyday life. We notice the contrast the moment we step out into the Belfast streets. It was comical to listen a few years ago to a Radio Four Interviewer struggling to elicit from the Buyer of a Belfast Fashion House the answer she wanted: "I suppose; do you mind; I don't know how to put this question but am I right in thinking that when you go out buying in stock you are always looking at the cheaper ranges, at the lowest end of the market?" To which the Belfast Buyer answered: "I don't know what you are getting at. Our customers expect me to stock nothing but the best." It is the same with the Ulsterman who does well in business. The first thing he does is to buy a Volvo or a BMW. Then he builds himself a grandiose house on a hill, surrounded by ranch-style fencing. What I have said about fine dress is no mere talking point, believe me, for we have been humiliated by it again and again. If at home in Laundry Cottage we prepare breakfast wearing old slacks and a jersey, our Ulster house-guests invariably come down in fresh crisp blouses and well-pressed skirts from the leading fashion houses.

The loss which Ulster people feel most acutely in England is the loss of conversation, of wit, of repartee, of "crack". While Ulster must pull up its socks in a lot of other ways this is one field in which it would be a tragic mistake to throw away the old natural indigenous gifts and aim for some sort of English politeness and restraint.

Again and again Ulster people score heavily in the arts of conversation and the colourful use of words. The Home Help who tells you she was so frightened that she was shaking like an ash-pan leaf. The fellow in the house to help with some repairs will advise you – when dealing with a trouble-maker – to treat him with ignorance. Or the woman in the wee Home Bakery selling you a big bag of lovely bread to take back to England: "It's a tarrible pity of them puir craythers in England with no dacent bread to eat, so it is. One thing annyway: if they ask yous about The Troubles, be sure and tell them that we are not all canniballs." Or the observer of the ups and downs of the Cold War who noted sadly that the world was not what it was and that even top Foreign Office diplomats were defecating all over Europe. Naive and gullible though the English are, they are I hope not so innocent as to believe that all such strange usages are unintentional.

Some of the sharpest wits we ever encountered anywhere were "High Heedy'ns up at Stormount", in other words Permanent Secretaries in the Ulster Civil Service, Brains of Britain, bi-linguists in English and Irish, Governors of the B.B.C., voluntary unpaid lecturers at Queen's, after dinner speakers greatly in demand. We could do with them here in stolid, honest, reliable old Westmorland.

Without wishing to complicate still further this already crowded picture of life in Ulster and in England (a sort of Hieronymus Bosch "Garden of Delights", I fear) I do feel I must warn unsuspecting Ulster readers of two further habits in England. One is the wide spread practice of social kissing; the other is the great prevalence of sexual jokes or innuendos in everyday conversation.

Here is an example of the sort of English I hear or read all around me in England every day, often uttered by educated and well-placed people. "I council you to do like I do and make less attempts just to militate your losses. That is the one and only criteria. In a Report out yesterday for example, 60 per cent of those questioned agreed with the proposition while only one-third disagreed. Less than one in ten had no opinion". Cruel, perhaps, but there it is, between you and I.

But be charitable. You have a name for charity in Ulster. All the world knows, or should know, that you have a better record in Ulster for giving to charity than many parts of England. There have been times when you have headed the league in the United Kingdom.

On a totally different side of life one is struck again and again by the widespread habit in England of people taking the name of the place they live in. As well as the obvious cases of Carlisle, Kendal, Preston, one keeps running across people charmingly called after a village – Brian Hutton, Stella Kirkby, Professor Adam Sedgwick, Nurse Bowness, Raymond Ousby, Fiona Cartmel, Audrey Newbiggin. I am still waiting to hear of Bella Bellarena or of Larry Limavady Junction.

Another aspect in which the English do better is in the marketing of fruit and vegetables. Not as good as mainland Europe, England nevertheless does provide more attractive produce than can generally be seen in Ireland, North or South. It is a shame that a community that is basically rural and agricultural still does so poorly. It is time for the present slight improvement to be pushed much further on.

Ah, but the bread. Forgive me for coming back to the subject again. Any day (if you are unlucky enough) you may see me on my hands and knees on the floor of any supermarket scrabbling along the bottom shelf hoping to find some sodas or wheatens or a bit of barmbrack or – oh dear, oh dear – what would I not give for an Ormo fruit loaf. When I told the Management at Marks and Spencer of my obsession they just said that I had, at any rate, given them all a good laff. They must be short of laffs.

On Telling People about Ulster

As an Honorary Member of the Royal Town Planning Institute I regularly read their journal and look in vain for any reference to Ulster, any report on what Town Planners are doing there, any criticisms of plans or planning decisions, any word of interesting appointments. I have only rarely seen any major reference even though a lot of important things are going on – just look at the Lagan banks or at the Forest Parks or at the simple way in which the horrid gated-security city centre has been converted into a pleasant place to stroll and sit in peace and quiet. The very system itself deserves to be studied as it presents, in working and living form, the only example in the Kingdom of a fully comprehensive regional planning authority that enjoys at the same time the direct backing of Central Government.

I recall having similar feelings of emptiness when I used to read the British Medical Journal, the Dental Journal, the Nursing Times and the professional journals of lawyers, architects, water engineers, highway engineers, local government officers and so on and so on. (No doubt some conscientious officer will now angrily draw my attention to a splendid article he once wrote; fine, I don't mind being corrected in public for I know that any correction will be welcomed by thousands of readers who share my disappointment and annoyance).

Why should there be so little news about positive events in Ulster?

I think I know some of the reasons. Ulster people have developed a false feeling of inferiority, a doubt whether any contribution from them would be worth making. Besides, they represent only one-fortieth of the total population of the United Kingdom and an even tinier fraction of the national wealth and economic activity and they feel that they ought not to intrude on the bigger scene. Most important of all, they know that the day their factual article is due to appear in some journal is likely to be the day on which the I.R.A. bring off some obscene bomb blast that dominates the news and overshadows all rational discussion.

Editors of journals in Great Britain are not without blame, either. They become paralysed when confronted with a decision about Ulster; they are obsessed with the fear of being caught up in some alleged sectarian accusation for they are so easily taken in by blarney.

But if their journals sell throughout the United Kingdom surely it is up to them to go out and hire reliable local correspondents. It can be done. Just look at The Independent or at Farming News.

This extraordinary fixation of the English with alleged sectarianism has to be tackled head on. I recall with amusement a B.B.C. Radio Four interview with the world-famous Belfast pianist Barry Douglas, when the silly interviewer – no doubt egged on by an even sillier producer – kept trying to stir up some controversy with which to entertain her listeners: "I don't know how to put this, do you mind if I ask, perhaps you would tell me, if you can remember, when you were training as a young man in Belfast, did you ever, I mean,

11

actually meet a Catholic?" Barry Douglas's reply was terse and to the point: "I attended the Belfast School of Music. All sorts were there – Catholics, Protestants, Jews. We were there to study music."

Or Seamus Heaney, the greatest poet of our day in the English language, when asked the same sort of stupid but intentionally divisive question, answered: "Of course I did. In rural County Derry we all lived together. The only difference I can remember as a boy was that we sold eggs to the neighbours and when the customer coming up the path was a Protestant my mother would look at herself quickly in the mirror, touch her hair and straighten her apron before opening the door". I hope I record fairly the gist of both interviews and convey the moral clearly, for I respect both men enormously. Two of the greatest.

To combat all those misunderstandings and displays of total ignorance we need far more reliable contact between Ulster and the wider world. Dr.Gordon Beveridge, present Vice-Chancellor of the Queen's University, is making a splendid effort to send interesting news about the University out to Graduates far and wide. His expanded annual letter makes stimulating reading in itself, with its vivid account, for example, of more and more productive co-operation between academic staff and innovative industry in Ulster.

"Partnership", the attractive journal promoted by the Industrial Development Board, is devoted to keeping interested people all over the world in touch with industrial changes and future possibilities in the Province. A most attractive production it errs just a bit on the side of presenting far too many photographs of men in good suits congratulating one another and bravely speaking up for Motherhood and Apple Pie. It suppresses any news of the political violence that afflicts industry and commerce in the Province. This is of course an intricate and sensitive problem. Terrorism is not their business. Why ought they to go out of their way to give the I.R.A. more of the "oxygen of publicity?" And yet everyone knows what is going on and what a burden it is; and it seems to me to be both naive and wrong to avoid the subject. One practical way of dealing with the problem in any Ulster publicity sheet is to high-light the successful way in which owners, with the willing co-operation of the trade unions, get on top of each disaster and quickly start work again. There could be many a good journalistic story there, with photographs of before, during and after.

Incidentally, on the back page of the 1991 issue of "Partnership" in 1991 the names of the editorial staff were listed: all five were women, a fact that is surely significant.

It was pretty chicken-hearted of Government to stop publishing that useful little news-sheet "Ulster Commentary". That was also a net loss because it did a lot of good in its albeit bland way and could easily have been improved.

People need facts if they are to speak up and talk to the world sensibly about Ulster. There are plenty of Ulster men and women in Great Britain, Europe and America (to go no further) who would gladly do what they could to help to project a picture of the real Ulster that they know and respect. They would not all agree; some would be more critical of Ulster attitudes than others; that is only to be expected. But I believe enough common ground exists between James Galway with his flute, Ken Branagh with his plays and films, Gloria Hunniford with her cheerfulness, Van Morrison with his extraordinary singing, John Cole with his political wisdom, Tom Paulin with his hard judgments, Bernard Davey with his homely weather forecasts – "there might be a wee break in the cloud between Bangor and Donaghadee" – Robert Ramsay with his European research, yes and even Georgie Best, the greatest British footballer of our time, and Hurricane Higgins to whom these dreary but highly-paid snooker players of to-day ought to be putting up a statue – in gratitude for all that he did for them when he introduced the game to the wider public in such dazzling style.

Experience has shown me that it is usually right to trust even the most unlikely people; clear-headed views can often burst out in unexpected places. Once, for example, in 1972, I was being introduced to the famous Irish film actress Greer Garson at one of those glittering celebrity parties in Georgetown, Washington D.C. When I spoke about Ireland, she told me how she had been approached a short time previously by a mindless Irish organiser for some "Irish" cause: "We're running a fund-raising dinner next Fall," he had said, "I'm sure we can count on you to support the armed struggle for freedom in the old country." "No, you can't!" was her snappy reply, as she told it to me, "That's not my Ireland. I don't see things that way. Get lost!".

All those men and women are part of Ulster. They are Ulster, for Ulster is a people more than it is a place. Once when agonizing over the old problem of whether Northern Ireland with its six Counties was claiming too much in taking on the more popular title: "Ulster" I consulted my life-long friend Jim Carney, Celtic Scholar and Senior Professor at the prestigious Dublin Institute of Advanced Studies. He answered me in some such words as: "Ulster always meant the people. They expanded and contracted over the centuries, sometimes over the whole northern part of Ireland, sometimes only over the north-east corner, Antrim and Down – like a bellows (that, I remember, was the word he chose). But Ulster was essentially a people. Far from claiming too much with the title Ulster, you could well be selling yourselves short!" In that sense I look on Ulster as embracing all her sons and daughters, all her friends and sympathisers, wherever they may be living and working. It was always so, to my mind. A generation or so ago I should have been looking to Louis McNeice, Robert Lynd, John Megaw, St.John Ervine or C.S.Lewis (of "Screwtape" fame):- we lived for many years on the Circular Road directly opposite the house "Little Lea" in which he had been brought up – and countless others to speak up and tell the facts about Ulster and about what the Ulster people have suffered from militant Republicans. Do not let yourself be cajoled into thinking that the present outburst of I.R.A. violence, so colourfully projected on T.V., is the first or only one. Do not overlook their six-year campaign of 1956–1962 which the Northern Ireland authorities dealt with on their own and neatly finished off; and do not overlook the fact that the Ulster political leaders then performed the remarkable feat- always overlooked – of restraining the loyalists from retaliating. Or any of the earlier outbursts of militant, anti-British action right back to 1641. One pair of old ladies on a lonely farm near Ballymena are still said to man-handle the dresser across the kitchen floor every night and wedge it against the outside door as a protection against invaders; they say they have done so every night since 1641. Ulster has manned one of the frontiers of the United Kingdom now for close on four centuries. The people there have made mistakes in plenty and they may not always have acted as nice, polite respectable English people would have done,

or imagine they would have done. After all, the English have not been tested
for a long time. Having now lived and worked among the English and heard
their views on "Blacks and Paks" I am not sure they would have behaved any
differently from the Ulster people who, for better or for worse, in plain fact
absorb the brunt of Republican aggression and violence before those afflictions
reach England.

Another group whom we foolishly neglect are those English professional
men and women who have spent some years in Ulster working at a hospital or
college or factory and then in the ordinary course of their careers have
returned to England. I meet them constantly in Cumbria perhaps socially,
perhaps when speaking to an audience or perhaps when conducting election
meetings in connection with the National Health Service. Once they hear my
unmistakable accent they go out of their way, without any prompting from
me, to come a long and tell me how much they enjoyed their time in Ulster,
how much the children benefited from schooling there and how keenly they
felt for what the local people in Eniskillen or Lisburn or Armagh are suffering.
The inner point, I always notice, is that their direct experience in Ulster has
made them immune to the usual blarney and beguiling misrepresentation. It
has been a bad blunder to neglect those people. All in all I have spoken to
something between fifty and sixty meetings in Cumbria and North Lancashire
on various aspects of real life in Ulster and always thought it worth doing –
whatever the audiences may have thought of me. To claim that English
people are not interested is, in my experience, simply not true. They are just
baffled and confused.

Some of the people best placed to convey to fellow citizens in Great
Britain something of what they found in Ulster are of course the Ministers,
past and present, of the United Kingdom Direct Rule team since 1972. With
an ear closely attuned to these matters I wait day by day to hear one of them
speak out. But they don't. I know for a fact that most of them found their time
at Stormont more enlightening and a lot happier than their friends at home in
England had gloomily predicted for them: "Banished to the salt mines of
Carrickfergus" or "Sent out there as a punishment for some misdemeanour".
And all of them found that they were enjoying far more political freedom in
their Ulster jobs than they might ever have expected to experience in
comparable postings in Whitehall. Apart from one splendid statement by the
unusual but estimable Peter Bottomly M.P. about the "superb" quality of the
Ulster Civil Service, I cannot myself recall any telling or penetrating analysis
from any of those Ministers speaking in the sense I am describing, still less
any useful, authoritative comparison between the way in which a neutral
problem is dealt with in Great Britain and in Northern Ireland. No doubt
they do what they can in private and they certainly produce a series of good
answers to Parliamentary Questions – in an empty House of Commons, alas –
but they do not seem to have seriously influenced public opinion in any
perceptible way. They are casting away a golden chance to consolidate opinion
in the United Kingdom. They have little to be proud of in that context. No
wonder Ulster is looked on as their political graveyard; they help to dig it
themselves. New thinking is urgently needed.

A valuable channel of information and advice about Ulster could be
created in the House of Lords if we were to elevate to that Chamber outgoing
"Heads of the Northern Ireland Civil Service". Few people can have deeper

knowledge of affairs in Ulster and fewer still can have closer experience of the impact of politics on administration and of administration on politics than those uniquely placed men. Here lies a real opportunity to contribute to top-level debate in Britain, to counteract blarney and to steady opinion. They are regularly knighted, as is right and proper, but a place in Parliament would be vastly more useful. And any objection on grounds of rank or precedence vis-a-vis Whitehall or St.Andrew's House would be of little weight compared with the national advantage of giving a platform to impartial, dedicated spokesmen from this sorely troubled and misrepresented region.

And what about all those advisory committees, consumer bodies, watch-dog organisations and so on? Post Office, Telecom, T.V., Radio , Air Travel? How many Ulster representatives are there across the board, swapping experiences and looking at practical problems both from the Great Britain and the Ulster point of view?

I am asking for more positive information in Great Britain and Europe about what actually is being achieved in practical ways in Ulster. What ought speakers or writers to say? Let them say what they like; they will do that anyway. But it is possible to supply them with facts to displace fiction. Professor Tom Wilson's fine book "Ulster: Conflict and Consent" could be a speaker's vade-mecum. Or the new "Northern Ireland Question: Myth and Reality" edited by Barton and Roche of the University of Ulster. And best of all a steady flow of factual material and impartial comment in a smart, up-to-date Ulster Bulletin sent to all who asked and who are ready to pay five pounds. I should be Subscriber No.1, just as I am Member No.1 of the "Friends of the Union" even though I have never belonged to a political party.

But even that is not enough. New thinking is needed. Some bigger aims need to be set to which all Ulster men and women could contribute and from which all would benefit. One of the tragedies inflicted on Ulster was the decapitation of society in 1972 after the abolition of Parliament and again later after the rejection of the Report of the Constitutional Convention in 1976. I smile wryly when I hear to-day the plea to local people to agree to form a new political assembly, made by the very people who abolished just such an assembly twenty years ago and humiliated its leaders. Whatever you may have thought of them, they were the freely elected leaders of the people within the democratic electoral system.

Let us therefore take it on ourselves to set some new goals.

Clean beaches? We have a string of gorgeous sandy beaches. Let us aim to make every one of them clean and fit to bathe in. "Every beach a bathing beauty". Or the water – we have plenty of it – let us aim for nothing less than 100% purity: "Every drop to drink !" Why not aim higher, set out to abolish pollution and start making Ulster "the green province", the emerald in the crown? Why not do more to reduce poverty, and bring the far-too-wide financial gap more into line with the remarkable absence of class consciousness in our society where we all speak with the same accent? Why not devolve functions from the statutory boards to the staggering array of willing volun-tary bodies in the field of social welfare?

Why not encourage our bigger Grammar Schools to set up or enlarge their boarding houses and then recruit the brightest "assisted pupils" from all over Great Britain? and from Europe? and from the world?

Or a brand new British College for Advanced New Farming, a sophisticated, post-graduate course specializing in the farming of the twenty-first century, in alternative forms of farming, organic culture, animal breeding, forestry, conservation? Farm tourism and so on? The Stormont Ministry of Agriculture would be admirably placed to start such an enterprise with its own veterinary research department, its own forestry department and its unique system of agricultural education at the University, the farm colleges and the advisory services. I can think of no other single body in the United Kingdom as well placed to give such a new thrust to agriculture as the Stormont Ministry. And I can see a brand new, purpose-built college complex rising up in Magilligan and looking out over the North Atlantic Ocean and the hills of Donegal.

Those are of course only my ideas, personal and no doubt foolish, impractical, unrealistic. As with any proposal relating to Ireland I can already hear cynics jumping up from behind every whin bush and arguing ever so eloquently: "It wouldn't work!"

What would work, then?

On Being an Instonian

When I heard the Chief Political Editor of the B.B.C. one afternoon quote the famous line from Robert Burns "A man's a man for a' that" and bring out the basic egalitarianism of the underlying truth that it contained, I thought that the line might well have serve d as a motto for my old school, Royal Belfast Academical Institution. Of course John Cole knew perfectly well what he was doing; as well as paying tribute to the poet Burns he was neatly linking up the whole body of feeling in Southern Scotland with the body of feeling that echoes it in Ulster – social equality, love of education, absence of class consciousness and so on.

I was struck, from my earliest days at Inst in the 1920s, by the extraordinary mixture of pupils all around me. Some were from the city, some from the country. Inst stood in the middle of the big city looking out on Wellington Place, Donegall Square and Chichester Street. Belfast was one of those cities with only one centre, obvious and unmistakable. The main roads all radiated from it. The trams in my day followed the same hub-and-spokes-of-the-wheel pattern, with every service route passing through the centre. In the broader setting of the Province Belfast stood likewise at the hub of the wider railway pattern: Belfast and Co Down Railway to Bangor, Donaghadee, Newtownards and even to Newcastle at the foot of the Mournes; the Great Northern to Lisburn, Lurgan, Portadown and again even to the same Newcastle; the Midland to Carrickfergus, Larne, Antrim and away to the North-West. The outcome was that even as a day school Inst drew its pupils from every corner of the city and from Counties Down, Antrim and North Armagh. Meehan lived right next to the school in College Square; Burns and Kane a few hundred yards away in Great Victoria Street; while Stevens and Gilmore actually travelled in every day from Newcastle by train, a distance of 36 miles each way. And Nesbitt from Goraghwood, Newry.

And now Maurice Hayes in his delightful Memoir "Sweet Killough" describes Barry Martin, wearing a yellow and black cap, going off every morning to Belfast by train from that remote County Down fishing village.

The geographical mix was strong; but the social mix was equally strong. There were boys the sons of judges, farmers, shopkeepers, bishops, professors, shipyard workers, linen lappers, labourers as well as my little group, the City Scholars, who benefitted from the generous arrangement under which the City Education Authority sent thirty of us – girls as well as boys – to the grammar schools of our choice, a sort of "Assisted Places Scheme" far ahead of its time. But that conveys little of the richness of the mixture. I think of the boy Rawsthorne with the Lancashire accent whose father had come over to play the piano at the Classic Cinema in those days of silent films. I think also of those intelligent Jewish boys from the successful merchant class of the Antrim Road.

In that melting pot social origins faded quickly. What mattered was how you got on in class, how you stood with your fellows, how well you did at

17

Rugby (and to a much lesser extent at Cricket) or in the play or the concert or simply what sort of figure you cut around the quad. What you were, not who you were. A man's a man for a' that.

The commonly held view in England that institutions and bodies in Ulster are all manned by raging Ulster bigots and bowler-hatted Orangemen could not be further from the truth. Inst in my day for example was staffed with senior masters from all over the British Isles and further afield – Brierley, Harriman and Darbyshire from Lancashire, Lawrie from Dumfries, Garrod, the Principal, from Kent, Carre from Rennes, Douglas from Greenock, Fitzgerald Studdert from Dublin and so on. If anything the popular criticism of our grammar schools then was that they looked too much to the outside world and trusted too little to local talent. These things go in cycles of course; I doubt whether many English men or women have been appointed as Heads in the last twenty years of I.R.A. activity and the turbulence which that has caused.

Add to those mixtures of pupils and staff a high standard of scholarship for its own sake and in particular of scholarship regardless of any examination syllabus. The old, old schoolboy trick of luring a master into a long digression so as to put off the moment when he would call for your homework succeeded well and gave us many a half-hour of stimulating monologue: Archie Douglas reciting Scottish Border ballads, Freddie Wright with hilarious tales of the antics of small banks in America, John Cowser on Italian opera, Johnny Pyper on the treatment of right and wrong in English literature: these turned out to be some of the high points in our real education. I pity all those prominent people in Britain who in their memoirs regret their school-days and deplore their schools.

And again an extraordinary dose of individualism among the teaching staff. It is hard to say whether this sprang from their diverse origins, or from the spirit of the times after World War I or from the tradition of the school right from its founding in 1810 or from the sheer fact that like attracts like and that an individualistic senior master will lean towards the individualist rather than to the conformist when making a staff appointment; but they really were a radical bunch in the 1920s. As it was neatly put by one master who happened to have taught as an assistant both in Campbell College out at Belmont and in Inst, the contrast could be seen most easily in the two staff rooms: at Campbell the atmosphere was that of a quiet, well-run club with copies of The Field lying around on deep arm-chairs and with a barrel of beer on tap; at Inst a wide-eyed young teacher bursting in and saying: "Wait till I tell you. I'm going to put on a new event with the Lower Sixth, a sort of dramatic protest and I need all you fellows to help."

It was just such activities that stimulated our minds and opened our eyes. A Shakespeare every Christmas without fail, a concert at Easter; a debating society that met once a week; in a word, a second curriculum that fully matched the academic one. And as John Grummitt, the Principal, put it once on Speech Day: "Hardly a term goes by without at least one group of boys coming to me and saying: 'We want to set up a new club (or whatever) and will you be President, please?'

The dull-looking "School News" reflects all of those thriving activities, term by term. And as the years have passed the range has widened so that now it reflects the interest of the boys in business activities, computers, social concerns and so on. Any Instonian wife or mother will confirm that once "School News" drops through the letter-box her man is lost to the household, deaf to all talk, far away in Paradise.

That brings us to the nub of the matter. Inst has a grip on us all. We may have been happy at Primary School; we may have grown up a lot at University; but Inst has by far the greatest hold on us, whatever our age, wherever we may be. The President of Belfast Old Instonians Association need only blow a trumpet in Princes Street to fill an Edinburgh banqueting hall; or in Piccadilly to fill a London hotel; or in Toronto; or in Cape Town; or now I suspect in Brussels. The appeal is irresistible.

Mind you, I could find fault with some of these old boy get-togethers if you were to press me. They attract the successful and the mutually admiring, they ignore the unsuccessful, the drop-outs, the unhappy ones, the very boys who once linked arms and shoulders with you in the scrum. There is room for fresh thinking. The functions are conservative to a degree that is no longer acceptable. Although I enjoy going to the Edinburgh dinners I find them grotesquely old-fashioned. My pleas go unheeded: switch to Glasgow, now a more interesting city than Edinburgh and much more in tune with life in Belfast; bring in wives and sweethearts – it really is offensive to cut them out of these male occasions and yet expect them to make tea somewhere else another day; give us a walk-about buffet rather than a starchy, sit-down, formal dinner where – as a retired master once put it to me rather starkly – "I am imprisoned all evening beside a boring little creep I couldn't thole when I used to teach him!".

In the course of a long and varied career I have had, like everyone else in a senior position, to offer appointments to all sorts of men and women, in all sorts of circumstances. In the same way when I was Chairman of the Board of Governors it fell to me several times to approach former pupils or parents and invite them to become Governors. Never, anywhere, have I felt such a surge of pride, pleasure and willingness to serve. And I was never let down. All threw themselves into the work of the Board. Attendance was remarkable. Every item was debated. Every Governor put in something from his business or professional experience. Every decision was closely monitored. Especially Rugby football for Inst was a Rugby school, fierce, committed, competitive. The Governors did little to conceal their distress when the School Fifteen failed to do well. They would have expected every Master to turn out on Saturday morning and coach Rugby, before anything else. They would put the Principal under pressure. Once, when Victor Peskett was reporting to them on a staff appointment he had made, I sensed from the chair that he was spinning out the teacher's qualifications a shade more than usual: "P.J.Smith, aged 25, a First in Modern Languages at Oxford, a Diploma in Education with Distinction from a Training College in London, some teaching experience in Northern France and in Southern Germany, ready to help with drama, interested in art as well, plays the oboe . . . " The Principal had hardly drawn breath when the inevitable question came from one of those determined men from the Shane Park Club on the Back Bench: "All very fine and dandy, I'm sure, but can he coach Rugby?" To which SVP replied icily: "Patricia Jennifer Smith is a woman."

I happened to be in the chair when we started to take serious notice of our long-term position and of the state of the school buildings. Scope for expansion was limited as Inst is on a tight, closely bounded inner city site. Perhaps, rather than tinker with old buildings that ran back a long time, some as far as 1810, we ought to move out to our beautiful playing fields at Osborne Park, build a new school there with plenty of space, in keeping with the educational needs of the future, contribute some bold architecture to Belfast, and flog the old place off as a super-market, so to speak, with a multi-storeyed car-park on the front lawn; and endow ourselves, for the first time ever, with a few million pounds in the Funds.

I was one of those in favour of the move. I saw the City Centre that I loved deteriorating before our eyes under I.R.A. bombing and becoming a sordid spectacle in the 1970s. The hub-and-spokes pattern of city traffic was being gradually relaxed, anyway, with modern bus routes criss-crossing each other and running in many directions. Even the railways were changing. Many pupils were being brought to school by car. There were now two Universities in place of one and a lot of new colleges spread around. The old certainties were going. We got to the stage of picking a firm of Architects and of starting to draw up dazzling new plans.

But we did not go ahead. We decided to stay at College Square in the centre of Belfast.

In anguish I rehearsed all those arguments privately one day to a distinguished Instonian, no less a person than a Supreme Court Judge. His reply was firm: "Yes John I agree with all your arguments for moving out. But if I had been on the Board at the time I should have voted against you!"

The influence of history and tradition and above all, I think, of presence proved too strong. Our position in the City and the Province rose above all questions of mere buildings and repairs. We could not become a suburban school. We had been founded clearly and deliberately as a liberal, non-sectarian city centre school away back under King George III – serving also for a time as a University College; we had kept our independence through all the generations, independence of spirit and style and, painfully, even of finance while still remaining firmly within the state system and its regulations and subject to inspection. We were a unique institution in so many ways. We stood for something important. We could be seen every day by van drivers, commuters, office clerks, shop assistants, housewives passing by: "That's the Inst" they would say over centuries as they glanced across our lawn at our famous Georgian front. They still do, thank goodness.

That's the Inst.

On Being treated for a Sore Back

I was in misery from about 1945 till 1985. Hardly a day passed in those busy active years of my life that did not bring a dull ache to my lower back or a heavy dragging feeling in my legs, each of which seemed to weigh a ton, or a sickening pain right across my back or a sharp jag around either or both of my sacro-iliac joints (those little knobs that stick out backwards from you pelvis about two inches east and west of the lower part of your backbone) or crippling sciatica or frightening lumbago; once in fact sciatica and lumbago together, a formidable combination.

I am ready to believe that my case was no worse and no better than the generality of sore backs that afflict the nation.

The fact is that I was examined, diagnosed and treated many times, over a stretch of forty years, with little effect or improvement. Then, a few years ago, I, the same person with the same anatomy and the same complaint was examined, diagnosed and treated with remarkable results and great improvement. I have been on the look-out for a chance to tell my story. Indeed I have felt a duty to pass on to other sufferers the gist of my experience. Several meanings of the word "Essay" now strike me as particularly fitting for my present purpose.

During those horrible forty years I stuck the pain as loyally as I could but felt forced once every four or five years to go and see my doctor. From that point on, each time, the process became an unvarying routine: "This really is too bad. We musn't let this go on. We'll get you to see a Specialist at once. Mr.So and So is the best man we have now-a-days in Orthopaedics." Mr.So and So, there were so many of them, and I was so fed up, that I have forgotten their names now. Anyway, he examined me with all the latest techniques and most sophisticated equipment and promptly prescribed: heat or heat and massage, pills, manipulation under anaesthetic or – I almost forgot – a corset. I think I had four corsets in all, prescribed by high level Consultants and fitted by trained, specialist providers under contract to the Health Service. Apart from giving me a nice warm feeling for a day or two, those treatments did no good. Looking back I now think that they were all a waste of time, money and effort.

Needless to say I did not leave it at that. Again and again I took the advice of friends and colleagues and in desperation went secretly to see some quack in a back-street. Belfast is full of boilermakers, rivetters and others from the Shipyard who claim to have a knack of curing ailments, sincere men, men with a high sense of moral duty who – I can vouch – refuse to accept any payment from the long queues of suffering men and women on their humble, well scrubbed doorsteps. Some put their thumb nail into your back, press until they hear a click and send you away cured and walking on air – for a day or two. Some favour the vinegar-and-brown paper recipe. One in the heart of the Shankhill advised me to lie on the floor at home, on my front, and get my wife to walk up and down my spine – in her bare feet, he added compassionately. Stiletto heels were in fashion that year.

For most of the time, of course, the pain was gnawing at me and dragging me down. I was driven into doing what little I could to help myself, relying partly on instinct and partly on a dim understanding of anatomy.

I would get up from my desk in the office – and there at once I would identify one of the biggest causes of the trouble, namely leaning over a desk for hours on end – and annoy my colleagues by walking around with my hands pressed into the small of my back. I would press my front forward and arch my back as fully as I could manage. Crude and instinctive, this technique nevertheless has turned out to be very much in line with the most modern advice from Physiotherapists: emphasizing lordosis or the natural curvature of the spine – to be quite clear, inward and forward to counteract the all-too-frequent slouch which so many of us slip into. If I passed under the branch of a tree or any overhanging structure – a children's climbing frame was always a welcome sight – I would reach up, seize the structure above my head and then let the full weight of my body swing from it. This produced instant relief and I now see that I was unknowingly performing a primitive if dangerous form of traction. A hard base to my bed, a solid set of one-inch planks, was probably the most effective single remedy that I devised for myself. More idiosyncratic remedies included stuffing a book inside the back of my trousers so as to help to keep the spine arched forward (one of the keys to relief). Starting with a simple paper-back (the first was "Twenty-Five", the autobiography of the precocious young Beverly Nicholls). I was quickly driven to something thicker and firmer – a hard-back novel. Then Nuttall's Dictionary. Then in utter distress I used my copy of Vanston's "Public Health", a huge, enormous hard-back text-book running to some nine hundred pages. I tried to go even further and use Vanston's "Local Government" but it ran to two stout volumes and the outer one kept slipping down and lodging itself in the leg of my trousers – an unhappy sight and a nasty encumbrance. In polite circles to-day that device would be known as a "lumbar roll".

Another helpful trick was to adjust the level of the position in which I was used to sitting and writing at a table – or, dare I mention it again, an office desk. The technique was to go around and find the chair with the lowest level of seat. Then raise the level of the table or desk by putting a wooden block under each leg or support. The combined effect was to increase the gap between seat and table-top and so force one to sit more or less upright. I still do this. Posture, I find, is all-important.

While these stunts were of some help, they brought no lasting benefit. Perhaps I did not persevere enough, perhaps I did not discipline myself firmly enough.

At last, in 1985, I made up my mind to tackle the horrible problem once and for all. Ransacking the libraries of Kendal and Lancaster I brought home no fewer than six books bearing on sore backs. I devoured them all and decided that the most useful for me was a book by Professor Malcolm Jayson of Manchester University and the Hope Hospital, their big man on Rheumatology but known popularly as the Professor of Sore Backs.

My own Doctor very kindly agreed to co-operate and referred me to the great man in Manchester. Malcolm Jayson found the solution.

Using no equipment or fancy gear he simply looked through me with his own X-ray eyes and acute perception, sized me up as a person and told me what I needed to do: loosen up my joints, strengthen my muscles, let the muscles do the work of holding my bones in place and make a proper job of it. Good-day to you.

A week in the beautiful rehabilitation hospital of Gisborne at Clitheroe in Lancashire taught me what to do in order to achieve these three simple aims. The staff there would have wished me to stay for several weeks – which would have been tempting – but I found the heavy daily fee far too dear by my modest standards. I just could not bring myself to spend that amount of money when I was not sick but strolling around each day in lovely gardens alongside a trout-stream in the beautiful Lancashire countryside (of which one otherwise hears or sees so little). So I stayed long enough only to learn some of the useful exercises from the excellent staff there and then for once in my life, more or less discharged myself.

Swimming, with additional exercises in the water, turned out to be the main course of treatment recommended to loosen my joints and build up my muscles. But remember, the third arm of the advice was to make a proper job of it. Since getting that splendid start I have attended the local swimming pool about twelve hundred times. We are lucky in Kendal to have a most attractive little hydro-therapy pool provided by voluntary subscription. My condition is now vastly improved. I know very well that I am not free from trouble. Three of the knobbles in my spine show signs of wear and tear which might be callously described as osteo-arthritis if one were disposed to use big words which, you will have noticed by now, I am not. My back could still give trouble. Those knobbles could strike me down any day. But the plain fact is that I am free from pain, can climb a mountain or, more important, go about my daily affairs without that dragging, aching, debilitating feeling I endured for all those terrible years. And if I do hurt myself, say by foolishly lifting a heavy weight from an awkward stance, I can shake off the pain in a couple of days by dint of exercise and fresh air; the same pain would have lasted weeks or months when I was ten, twenty or forty years younger.

And it helps if one can keep down one's weight. The surprising geometry of the body seems to mean that one of the worst things for a bad back is a big belly. Diet is crucial. Bit by bit my diet has changed until it is now about 90% vegetarian, with a couple of helpings of fish a week and with meat only on odd social occasions for the sake of social ease and convenience.

People differ. Cases differ. I do not for one moment presume to say that what has been helpful to me will be helpful to anyone else. The advice I do pass on is advice in favour of thinking about one's problem, reading about it, asking questions of the Doctors and generally taking time to apply one's mind actively to the problem. In any case the mind has a big part to play. Thinking positively and optimistically can help a lot.

I do not feel in any way resentful against those Doctors who wasted all those precious years. I do not blame them. I do however, think that the experience I have described here may underline the danger of the profession letting itself sink into the rut of stereotyped thinking. To explain what I mean: why was I sent in every case to an Orthopaedic Surgeon? Why never to a Physician? Or to a Rheumatologist? Or even to a Psychiatrist? Or to a Consultant in Physical Medicine?

Now, looking back, I see that I have myself to blame for forty years of pain. I ought to have broken ranks and thought out some fresh courses of action for myself. Of course I was leading an exceptionally busy life at work and at home, with a large family, with a big garden and with many pressing outside interests. There was no such thing as a little hydrotherapy pool nearby, with nice warm water and quiet atmosphere. I did not have the time, or I did not make the time, to read a lot of medical books on the subject of sore backs, think deeply about them, travel seventy miles to see a particular Physician and then go on to swim in a pool three times a week. I just struggled on from day to day. But I shall know better next time.

On Religious Divisions

A moderate man, indeed I might call myself an extreme moderate, trained to look at every problem in a balanced way I allow myself two whole-hearted convictions, unbalanced, unqualified, unmitigated.

One is against the death penalty in law. Full stop. No further argument.

The second is against the use of religious denominations in political life in Ulster, against describing people publicly according to religious affiliation and against talking about Protestants and Catholics in reporting terrorism.

Let religion and religious affiliation remain a personal and sacred matter and let them be taken out of politics.

Brought up on the streets of Belfast and the lanes of County Londonderry I know perfectly well the divide that exists. And I know that the divide is present in the minds of the people. And there are a few people – not many – who feel strongly on the theological arguments involved, on both sides. And I know only too well that there is a tendency, an attraction indeed, even a bit of good-natured fun, in referring to the other side as "Prods" or "Papes". But those become all-too-handy labels.

Religion is not the heart of the matter. The division within Ulster is not about religion. It is about politics, about nationality, about belonging, about passports, about flags and emblems, about territory, about anniversaries. The quite separate conflict between the I.R.A. and H.M.Government of the United Kingdom is something different again and has nothing to do with religion either. It would be hard for cynics to blame the bombing of the Queen's Horses in Hyde Park or of an army barracks in Germany on religious sectarianism, though I know some who would have a good try. Finally and conclusively the friendly working co-operation of the various Church leaders in Ulster, displayed again and again, makes it quite wrong to talk of "a religious war".

Besides, His Holiness the Pope when visiting Ireland in 1979 surely settled the argument by making his definitive pronouncement: This is not a religious problem but a political one.

And yet the outside world swallows all the blarney about an old-fashioned religious war and about total segregation.

New thinking is needed.

Remove the question about religion right out of the official Census Form and Census Returns. Of all the questions that are not needed in Ulster, not helpful, not constructive, that one is the leading contender for abolition. Besides, it has become a useless question and yields a meaningless set of statistics ever since Government relented to the extent of making it optional in the 1971 Census. More and more people very sensibly refuse to answer and thus give a silent lead to the politicians.

Religious affiliation has in any case become a misnomer. Church attendance is high but so also is Church non-attendance. Many so-called Loyalists in East Belfast branded as extreme Protestants "go no road on Sunday" and

25

"never darken a church door". The feelings, then, of genuine believers and worshippers when they hear of "Protestant" violence or "Catholic" retaliation can well be imagined; those feelings merit some protection.

The myth of one huge Protestant bloc staring eye-ball to eye-ball at another huge Catholic bloc is also far from the truth. In a fascinating paper published in "Myth and Reality" in Britain in 1991, Professor Fred Boal and other academics identify no fewer than thirty-six different Protestant denominations in Belfast alone and then go on to analyse the differing attitudes and responses of all those denominations to various political and social problems. There is no one Protestant bloc. And what about the Quakers? And the Jews?

Catholics are of course not split up in the way that Protestants are, for they belong to a much more homogeneous Church. But changes have taken place there, too. Church observances have dropped; and as one devout Catholic woman said to me at one of those Peace Rallies we used to attend: "Och sure since Vatican II many of us feel we are all more or less Protestants now".

And there are, I should reckon, head for head, vastly more ecumenical moves and joint services in Ulster between Catholics and Protestants than there are in Great Britain between Christians and Jews, Christians and Muslims, Muslims and Jews.

Published Government statistics of religious affiliation, besides being faulty and otiose, in fact serve a negative end, supplying bigots with all-too-handy ammunition, district by district, worse still electoral area by electoral area.

Newspapers and Broadcasters report: "A Protestant was shot in North Belfast last night"; "Two Catholic youths were killed in an ambush in West Belfast". What can the effect of such reporting be other than the keeping of a score-sheet, the creation of league tables, and the urge to score again? My father, a convinced liberal, used to comment to us around the kitchen fire on the shootings of the 1922 Civil War, with heavy irony: "I am disappointed to see in the League tables to-day that Chelsea failed to score a goal this week-end – sorry, I meant of course the Catholics".

I am convinced that the reporting of terrorist deaths by so-called religious affiliation is positively harmful and leads directly to still more deaths. Less harm would be done, less bitterness stirred up, more human sympathy created if Press, Radio and T.V. could be persuaded to describe the unfortunate victim as a taxi-driver, a breadman, a milkman, a door-keeper, a census enumerator, a father, a daughter – and leave it at that. This is an urgent matter and I plead openly for a Concordat between the Authorities and the Media. It need not go so far as to involve censorship and prohibition. Mature Press and Broadcasting Commissions could surely devise a workable plan if they put their minds to it.

Strangest of all is the well-meaning drive by Direct Rule Ministers to try to secure the laudable aim of a better distribution of jobs between Protestants and Catholics in industry, commerce and the public sector through the operation of Fair Employment. Even granted that its aims must be long-term, the drawbacks seem to me to outweigh the benefits.

I would abolish the arrangement at once and put Members and Staff to work on the really worthwhile task of expanding business and stimulating small enterprises in strife-torn areas ravaged by the I.R.A, those terrible street corners lovingly depicted on television. The strenuous and dedicated efforts of the former Ministry of Commerce and L.E.D.U. (Local Enterprise Development Unit) to induce industry to go to those difficult areas ought to be taken up and pursued with the vigour which that daunting task requires. That is where work is badly needed for a host of reasons. Providing more jobs provides more chances for everyone than Fair Employment can ever do. The basis on which the idea is founded seems faulty to me. Employers are forbidden by law to take religion into account when recruiting staff and yet afterwards they are liable to be publicly pilloried for not achieving a proper balance in their workforce. How is "balance" to be read? asks Professor Tom Wilson, Fellow of University College Oxford and Adam Smith Professor at Glasgow, in his well-researched and extremely reasonable book: "Ulster; Conflict and Consent". Balance in the whole community? Balance in the whole working population? Balance in the local area concerned? Balance in the working population holding the appropriate qualifications? From direct personal experience I would add the most telling test of all: Balance in the numbers of qualified people actually applying.

How is an employer to know for sure what religion an applicant belongs to? Or in to-day's world whether he belongs to any religion? Or, even more apt, whether he wishes his religious beliefs to be known and recorded and then used in some polemic?

In the old old days an employer was said to be able to tell by asking the innocent question: What school did you go to? But there were always some interdenominational schools. I was at one started in 1810. In modern times there have been Catholic parents who chose to send their children to a so-called Protestant School just to spite an arrogant Bishop. And there are now springing up more interdenominational schools. Some applicants will be applying from Great Britain. What then? Some will have been brought up in Great Britain and are now living in Ulster. What now? Some indigenous Ulster parents, Catholic as well as Protestant, will have sent their children to school in England – e.g. Rossall, or in Wales e.g. Howells, or in Scotland e.g. St.Leonards. How go? I was amused to read in the factual Answer to a Parliamentary Question on 20 February 1992 that even the well-placed and self-conscious Equal Opportunities Commission were unable to tell the religion of all of their own direct employees.

In a solemn, lengthy study of the Ulster Civil Service – which came out with a good record, I am proud to say, firmly and finally disposing of long-promoted and spiteful calumny – the sleuths were driven in the end to "attribute" religion to applicants and to "allocate" other applicants to particular religions. Thank you very much. That was jolly decent of them.

The comparison sometimes made with measures to cope with racial equality or equality for women is fundamentally misleading as they deal with charac-teristics of a nature totally different from personal religious belief and prac-tice in a rapidly changing world.

It is the general experience that all unpopular policies sooner or later need intense bureaucratic controls to sustain them. That is happening with Fair Employment; imposing an added burden on employers, a burden that, as Tom Wilson points out, will do little to encourage outside firms to set up in Ulster.

Employment quotas have been ruled out, wisely. Merit is the only test, for the moment: education, qualifications, experience, character and so on. Or nearly the only test for there surely must be one other test that any responsible employer must apply in Ulster after seventy years of terrible experience: Is the applicant for the job of door-man a security risk? If the employer does not satisfy himself on that, literally vital, test and his factory is then blown up as "an inside job", what will his other workers say to him? What will the Police say to him? What will he say to himself?

In a situation of unemployment, in what is called a zero-sum situation, recruiting one worker to satisfy some vague concept of balance is likely to mean the sacking of another.

Balance, whatever that may mean, can best be achieved where and when you have an expanding labour force. A renewed crusade is needed to get jobs into Nationalist areas, a crusade led by some vigorous, unconventional local Ulster men and women determined to succeed.

I find it hard to leave the issue there. If it is a fact, as Professor Paul Compton, Director of the School of Geosciences at Queen's reports indirectly in a closely researched article on "Employment Differentials", that both the Queen's University and the University of Ulster are believed to have been "exposed" for failing badly to reach "balanced" employment, then we are up against really hard facts.

Here we have two British Universities, staffed by high-level academics from all over the British Isles and further afield, strictly following the best British University recruitment policies and yet ending up – after twenty years of direct British Rule and influence – with an "unbalanced" work force. Clearly there must be other reasons and other forces at work.

The day that statistics in academic appointments are treated as more important than merit, we are done for.

But it does not need profound investigations and statistical analyses to prove what is obvious: Fair Employment is throwing the emphasis on the wrong approach, the approach that points backwards rather than forwards, the very approach which decent, thinking Ulster men and women want to get away from: the use of religion as an instrument of public policy. Any such approach, no matter how nicely presented, is bound to prove divisive and corrosive. Just as the unlamented Anglo–Irish Agreement of 1985, guaranteeing the Republic the right of interference on behalf of Catholics in Ulster was seen to be deeply divisive – and corrosive – from the very day it was signed. I find it hard to credit that so many politicians should have welcomed two such big steps clearly and obviously likely to divide rather than unite. I repeat again and again that what we need are approaches that look ahead, that stress expansion, enterprise, education, training, hard work, co–operation, and that are calculated, planned and executed to unite the people rather than to go on counting religious heads and carrying forward the tensions of the past. New thinking must oust the old thinking as I say again and again and again.

On Coming to the Fair

456 Malone Road
Belfast 7

My dear Mary,

You have talked often enough about coming over here to stay with us for a few days but so far you have never managed to get yourself organised, have you? This morning the Programme for the Queen's Festival came through the post and it struck me that this might tempt you. It runs for three weeks in November and I remember you saying that that was your slackest time. So why not give it a try? You'd love it.

Something for everyone, as they say. John Lill will be playing Brahms and Barry Douglas – the local boy made good – will be on his favourite Russians. No James Galway this year, I am afraid – he can always pack them in. But all the big musical events are so heavily booked that I had better get on the ticket trail right away. Surprisingly the tickets are done strictly in order of application, by computer actually, so there are no strings I can pull if we come late. As you never seem to get the R.S.C in your neck of the woods, this will be your big moment for they are doing a sort of Marlene Dietrich show "The Blue Angel". That will be up your street. The thing at the Grand Opera House, the Hamburg Ballet, will give you a chance to see that palace of wonders, our Frank Matcham gilt-and-crimson theatre complete, would you believe it, with elephants looking down on you from every side. Bombed twice by the I.R.A. but still going strong like the big Hotel next door. We must take you there for a meal one day, bombed twenty-nine times, they say. And you may even catch a glimpse of The Phantom of the Opera drifting around the theatre coulisses (that's our little private joke). And there are masses of shows all over the town, as well as the main events in and around the University.

Some of the best fun comes late at night, at the Guinness Spot or the Harp Folk. "Turn Down the Lamp" was a scream two years ago with Joe McPartland and an extraordinary character Sam McAughtry slanging each other with folksy jokes in the local dialect, laced with odd musical items by chaps from the B.B.C. But success went to their heads and they more or less repeated themselves last year without bringing in enough new material. That's the price of success if you know what I mane. But there I go again. This place takes you over and swallows you up after a couple of years, I reckon. But I wouldn't live anywhere else now. Ireland absorbs the invader, they say.

Knowing your liberal prejudices I can assure you on oath, before you begin to ask, that the whole Festival is completely non-sectarian. Actually – it wouldn't have occurred to me before I came here, what is it, three years ago now – but I shouldn't be surprised if there will be as many Papes as Prods on the stages this year. So you can relax. They're coming in the windows.

What's more, they're coming up in droves from Dublin and Cork for the chance of performing here. They love coming to this event. One of the nice things here, so different from England, you get to meet the artistes and hear their crack. You wouldn't believe it but they all say that the Belfast audiences are the best to play to. Billy tells me that it was always so. In the old days Frank Benson and Charles Doran gave far more farewell performances here than anywhere else. But, as Billy says, there is an extra ingredient now, because of The Troubles – see how I drop into the local lingo? – Belfast audiences are doubly glad to see any of the big touring companies braving the bombs and do them proud with a tremendous welcome.

Are you still as doe-eyed as ever about Irish Unity and all that nonsense as you used to be? You will find that I have cooled off. Living and working here makes you shed your old studenty notions and face reality. Anyway I am thinking of taking you down to Dublin for a couple of nights to see the theatres there, though with so many of their performers coming North we may not need to.

How is your own Drama Club getting on? The last I heard was that you were putting on a J.B.Priestly or was it a John Van Druten? How daring! If we can get ourselves sorted out – Billy is so unreliable about time-keeping as he always seems to be going out on Army patrol as soon as he comes home from work – I might take you to one or two of the local amateur clubs here, Bart's maybe or the rising phenomenon the Osborne Players. You'll find quite a difference. The amateurs here are much less fussy about polishing up their sets or their costumes than your clubs are but the acting is terrific and so is the producing. It will open your eyes. Some of the best things I have seen on any stage, anywhere, were "O'Flaherty VC" done by Bangor one sunny Saturday afternoon and "The Mad Woman of Chaillot" by Belfast Drama Circle – tremendous. It's a pity you won't catch the Amateur Drama Competitions; they reach a sort of orgasm in May with dozens of lively clubs competing their heads off to get to the Finals at the Opera House, having tholed some terrible slatings from an assorted bunch of bewildered Adjudicators from across the water as we say, (one blithely contradicting the other). The best night ever at the Finals was the famous Saturday night when Dundalk put on that old favourite by J.B.Keane "Many Young Men of Twenty Sailed Away", bumpety-bump, bumpety-bump. A sort of corny musical tear-jerker about emigration to England but it had the whole packed Opera House rocking, joining in the singing and actually anticipating the tunes. And the wretched Adjudicator had the gall to mark Dundalk down on that account! My blood boiled! Another injustice!

So – book yourself on a plane at Blackpool Airport and I'll gather up what's left of you at Sydenham. No trouble, the Airport's right in the City here. For anysake don't be wearing those awful purple slacks that you seem to live in. All the women here dress so sharply. If you do need to smarten yourself up a bit, Mary, I'll chaperone you to Renee Meneely's or some other fashion house around Donegall Square and get you kitted out decently.

And don't imagine you'll escape without a dose of the local hospitality. Are you still on the slimming jag? Billy has something like a hundred relations – at the last count – and a lot of them will expect you to call for a nice cup of tea that will turn out to be a sit-down supper with big fozy six-inch sandwich cakes and ham and cream and fruit loaf and everything.

That's it. Be ready for the worst. Give me a buzz.

Yours ever

Marge.

On Some Ulster-Scots and their origins in Scotland

I wish to recount briefly the results of some work I did in 1959–61 on the background of my family in the Limavady-Magilligan-Dunboe area of County Londonderry. The work was quite ordinary and the family unremarkable. When I came back to the subject twenty years later I made use of new material and better facilities, got some expert help and was able to look at my problem in a broader perspective.

It is only in the third phase (1985–87) that I have opened up new fields. I have been trying to see whether I could trace my people and their friends and neighbours (North Derry Ulster-Scot Presbyterians) back to their origins in Scotland. This turned out to be a fascinating experience and I believe a unique one.

The fourth part recognizes that while I may have managed to find some patterns of movement by modest farmers and tradesmen from southern Scotland to County Londonderry I have not been able to complete the task in terms of named individuals, places and dates. The task is beyond me (and beyond any single-handed amateur, I suspect) and so I finish by suggesting that more could be achieved by a professional team of historians and genealogists; and with several benefits.

PART I

The Early Work

My early work in 1959–61 was greatly helped by the fact that all four grandparents lived in north Derry and that, with their friends and neighbours, they were deeply rooted in that area. They were Presbyterians and small tenant farmers; they formed part of a homogeneous society. That greatly reduced the amount of my travelling in fieldwork and kept the scope of necessary documentary research (both in the North and in Dublin) within reasonable bounds. On the other hand, of course, the disadvantage was that such a static rural pattern of tight-lipped, parsimonious farmers produces little in the way of letters, diaries, portraits, pedigrees or the other hard material that a family possessed of land, titles, military connections or professional qualifications normally accumulates.

The well-known sources provided the basic material: the Valuation of Tenements 1858–64 (the only surviving section of which relates to Co. Londonderry); the Census 1831; the Tithe Applotments 1826–33; the Flax Seed Premium Scheme 1796; the Religious Census 1766; the Londonderry Walk 1740; the Hearth Money Rolls 1663; and the Muster Rolls of Sir Robert McLellan and Sir Thomas Phillips, presumably 1630 or possibly earlier. An energetic programme of visits to thirty-nine graveyards and much careful combing through countless church records contributed a lot. Interviews with local people (though time-consuming) also helped. Published books were useful in building up a picture of the geographical and social background but (as I was disappointed to find again and again) they provided practically nothing on family detail.

Overall I enjoyed no special luck, no chance finds, no 'bundle of old letters up in the attic'. In plain words the effort consisted simply of a great deal of hard work. Nevertheless the results were substantial.

Oliver

The main stem of the Oliver family was traced right back, with a pretty high degree of assurance, to the earliest days of the Plantation under King James I. The homestead was without doubt Derrymore-Derrybeg, two miles north-east of Limavady, a comfortable farm of good land, fine trees, rich orchards, trout streams and eventually a valuable clay brickyard. An original lease of 25th February, 1692 is extant (clearly the first fruits of the Williamite Accession). Earlier than that the Olivers were seen to be busy as Recorder and as Chamberlain of the Borough of Newtownlimavady in the seventeenth century. And the evidence is strong that those two men — James and John Oliver — were descended from a James and John Oliver whose names appear in Muster Rolls of 1630 (or earlier); and according to family tradition they came over from Scotland with other supporters of Sir Robert McLellan, later Lord Kirkcudbright.

One sees the Olivers as well set up and literate, able and free to play their part in public life over the centuries and contributing their share of venturesome young people going out to America in the waves of Ulster Protestant emigration in the mid 1700s.

While the Derrybeg Olivers formed the main stem, two other broad branches have been clearly traced: the Olivers at Dowland and Grannagh in Aughanloo, a mile north of Limavady; and those at Drumsurn, Cloghan and The Maine a few miles south of the town and further up the fertile valley of the River Roe. All in all, a substantial body of Olivers married repeatedly into the local society and fully identified with it over three of four centuries.

Sherrard

Our mother's family, the Sherrards, have farmed in Magilligan (down on that extraordinary flat raised-beach of sand and grass lying between Lough Foyle and the Atlantic Ocean) since the end of the eighteenth century at least. Information about the Sherrards since 1780 or so is abundant and consistent. Earlier than 1780 it is abundant but scattered and inconsistent. The evidence, and there is plenty of it, suggests that they moved down to Magilligan from that hilly area of Sistrakeel and Drumraighland (a few miles south of Ballykelly) in the eighteenth century, having lived there for a hundred or even a hundred and fifty years.

The difficulty which besets any research into the Sherrards arises from the name itself. For the past two hundred years or so they have called themselves Sherrard and they so appear in all written records. But in the Magilligan vernacular they are known universally as Shearer, or even as Shirer. In all the local records I have seen from the seventeenth and early eighteenth centuries

Shearer is the form commonly used, or occasionally Shirer or other variants. From my close study since 1959 of masses of evidence I cannot bring myself to conclude that there were two separate and distinct families in the one small area. I am satisfied that they were all one. In so far as the Shearer form predominates in the seventeenth century records, then to my mind that tends to confirm the Scottish origins, for Shearer was a prevalent name in Ayrshire and wherever else in southern Scotland sheep-rearing and the woollen trade flourished. Sherrard on the other hand is an English name, meaning the bright one or the very bright one (according to Rainey and Wilson: *Dictionary of British Surnames*); and I have seen nothing whatever through the four centuries to connect the family with English origins. The family has seemed to me to be in every case sense Scottish in character and associations. On a further small but significant point they were always able to see the Scottish Isles from Magilligan on a clear day.

Morrell

My father's mother was Martha Morrell born 1829, died 1909. She came from a large, well-known and well-established family in Dunboe, Castlerock. They have been relatively easy to trace, in themselves. For one thing they were Covenanters, belonging to small devout congregations conscious of their own separateness. For another, they farmed in a fairly big way, moving from one holding to a better one in the Knocknogher-Ballywildrick area, and leaving some records in the form of registered leases. They gave rise to no fewer than seven Ministers of the Church and that of course guaranteed some reliable records. In addition they set up some of the most handsome gravestones, with the clearest and most elegant lettering that I found in the whole area. There was no difficulty in getting back to the early eighteenth century, with less coherent but still numerous indications in the seventeenth.

The recurring problem in researching the Morrells was of yet a different kind. As well as with the Morrells in Dunboe, mentioned above, we also had clear associations with an equally strong, equally well-established clan of Morrells on the other wing of our north Derry area, that is to say around Terrydremont a few miles south of Limavady (whereas Dunboe lies well to the north-east of the town). There seemed to be no connection between the two; and each stoutly protested that as it spelt the name with one 'r' while the other spelt it with two 'r's, there could not possibly be any connection. (This was typical of a general problem that dogged my early work as I did not wish, at first, to hurt the susceptibilities of my close living relatives who were perhaps not too keen on having much to do with other branches from whom they have become cut off through change of religion, bad times, illegitimacy or whatever).

McMullan

My mother's mother was Rosanna McMullan (1852–1930) from The Glebe, Dunboe. It proved possible to take her family back, with fair assurance, to Daniel McMullan (1765–1820) and even to Gilbert McMullan listed in the Londonderry Walk of 1740 — suggesting a lifespan of possibly 1700–1770 or thereabouts. I was not able to link these McMullans back to a known Daniel McMullan whose will was proven in 1630, though the presumption was there.

The problem here was of yet a different kind again. It lay this time in the great number of Mullans, McMullans and O'Mullans in the north Derry area and in the difficulty of keeping a track of any one line of descent in what is certainly 'Mullan territory'. Nothing in genealogy is simple; and a seemingly welcome abundance of names can actually become a trouble.

These 1959–61 Papers

Although I knew very well that this early and rather hurried work of mine was far from complete I sensed that it had some value even if only for the many obscure references and local sources, for the warnings about time lost on false trails and for the frank recording of the personal experiences of someone working in the 1960 years — I therefore decided to lodge my papers as they stood (incomplete and no doubt faulty) with the Public Record Office of Northern Ireland and some libraries in order to make sure they would not be lost but would be available to others. I have been pleased to hear from time to time that many readers have found them helpful and even amusing.

PART II

The Second Phase

When I took up the search again in the early 1980s I found that the facilities had improved greatly. The new PRONI was an immeasurably better place to work in than the old rooms in the Law Courts Building in May Street, staffed by a man and a boy (though one must always add the admirable Miss Embleton).

Conscious always of the amateurish, part-time nature of my efforts I went out of my way this time to enlist the help of the Irish Genealogical Association and was lucky to have the services and advice of their senior professional researcher, Mrs Marie Wilson. Her review, while producing much new material for me, served to confirm the general trend of my early researches and to assure me that I had not been overlooking anything of importance in the conclusions I had drawn. Another benefit of this return to the problems of our family history after twenty years was that I felt able to stand back and look at some of the earlier difficulties in a new and broader light.

Spelling

Spelling of family names, for example, had originally worried me a lot. From training in other disciplines one is conditioned to observe the fine differences, to note them carefully and to draw appropriate distinctions from them. But that is an unreal pursuit in dealing with family names before the end of the nineteenth century. Time and time again I came across discrepancies that overrode all such conscientious distinctions: for example, Douglas on one headstone and Douglass on another stone within the same burial plot in Balteagh in Lislane. Not only that but one and the same headstone clearly records the burials of two sons of Joseph Douglass: Robert Douglass of Farlow in 1914 and James Douglas of Maine in 1927. Or again, at Bovevagh this time, Edward Wray and Wm Ray. Or at Largy, Dunsceith and Dunceith, Flemming and Fleming.

Even greater discrepancies occur in the main family names with which we are concerned in this study. The trivial point which sought to distinguish one family of Morrell from another on the score of one 'r' or two pales away when set against the many firm authentic variants of that family name which I have been able to record even within the one household. On the Marriage Certificate of my grandmother Martha Morrell dated 20th November, 1849 the name is spelt twice as Morell and twice as Morrell on the same entry and within a few centimetres. But worse is to come. I have assembled altogether no fewer than twelve variants in our small area: Murril, Morrell, Maurrell, Murrel, Morell, Murell, Murrial, Murriel, Murral, Murial, Murile, Murrile. What price one 'r' or two?

A similar range of variants occurs with Sherrard; Sherrar, Sherra, Sherrer, Sherer, Sheerar, Sherar, Sheror, Sherrid, Shearer, Sheirer, Shirer — all in our small area. Who is prepared to convince me that my grandfather (one of the grand old men of Magilligan, as his Obituary Notice in the Northern Constitution put it) Henry Sherrard was not the same man as I heard recalled with affection in Ballymaclary as 'oul' Henery Shearer'? Or that Samuel Morrell of Ballywildrick was not 'oul' Sam Murial', as Mrs Maxwell of Agincourt Avenue and formerly a Morrell of Dunboe put it to me.

Then there is the pitfall of location and the tendency of one branch to disown any connection with a kindred group of the same name living but a few miles away. In my earlier work this not only confused me but actually distracted me from thoroughly investigating the latter group. It was only on my second set of studies that I felt able, as with spelling, to take a detached view and look at all those people objectively.

Here were people of the same family name, bearing the same or similar Christian names; tenant farmers, educated, literate middle-class; Presbyterian or near variant; corresponding roughly in time-spans; burying their dead in nearby or even in the same graveyards; living out their lives a few miles apart in the same parish or contiguous parishes, and looking to the same small market town of Newtownlimavady for their commercial activities. I have come to look on my earlier fine, small-minded distinctions as simply laughable. I am now satisfied that such groups were all of one blood. Any other conclusion would be much less plausible.

If one still hesitates, then a useful test to apply in such a situation is the negative test, that is to say to take some standard document such as a Census Return or the Flax Seed Premium or a Valuation List, apply it to a quite separate parish such as Aghadowey or Glendermott twenty miles off but still within the same county and check the result. The absence there of Oliver or Sherrard (or whatever) will vividly confirm the presumption of consanguinity between groups (within the smaller area) that one may have been earlier misled into treating as quite separate families.

In this situation (and subsequent work described below) I have adopted my own rough-and-ready six-fold test by which to judge the likely relationship of people of the same, or nearly the same, family name, discovered in any particular district: location; time; prevalent Christian names; religion; occupation; social and educational standing. I commend this to others as one useful technique.

To return to the family history itself I am now as satisfied as it is possible to be in these difficult matters in Ireland that I have accurately traced the

Olivers back to about 1660; the Sherrards to 1655; the Morrells to about the same period and the McMullans to around 1700 — with in all four cases indications (disparate but each in itself authentic) of relationships going back to dates as early as 1630, 1617 or even possibly 1613. In other words our records have proved to be fairly reliable and reasonably consistent back as far as 1700 or 1680 but certainly not back into the earlier part of the seventeenth century. Given the turbulent history of Ulster in that century this conclusion will hardly come as a surprise to anyone.

Conclusion to this Second Phase

I do not think I can usefully pursue these researchers any further. The law of diminishing returns eventually asserts itself. I content myself, in this aspect of the work, with having provided Amy Oliver of Bromley, Rachel Fenn of Orpington, Anthea Kennedy of Deanfield, Francesca Balke of New York State, Eve McClure of Norfolk (and all the other young ones of today's generation) with eight, nine or ten generations of Ulster ancestors deeply rooted in our beloved County Londonderry. But I am fully aware that other family historians have done as well or better.

PART III

Scotland

So far the work had been, as I have said, ordinary and unremarkable. In 1985 I decided to try something much bolder. My people in north Derry had been in the Ulster-Scot or Scotch-Irish tradition and I am thinking not only of our direct ancestors but also of their close friends and neighbours of long standing: in and around Limavady itself there were Connell, Long, Irwin, Drennan, Douglas, Shannon, Trotter and Robinson; and in Magilligan Conn, Allison, Morrison, Linton, McCracken. The general belief was that they had come over from Scotland as part of the planned migration under King James I, perhaps as early as 1617 or 1618 and certainly by about 1635 or so. They were Presbyterians or Covenanters. They sang from the Scottish Psalter. Their churches were simple barn churches and their Assembly was closely linked with the Assembly of the Church of Scotland. Many of their Ministers over the long generations had been trained in Scottish colleges. Prudent Ministers economically exchanged pulpits during the summer holidays. Our people spoke (perhaps not in Limavady itself but certainly in Magilligan and Dunboe) with a most pronounced Scottish accent. They could quote at length from the poet Burns. At a political level the Ulster-Scot heritage was lauded and the Ulster-Scot origins of twelve or thirteen Presidents of the United States of America were widely advertised.

I therefore assumed, perhaps naively, that it ought to be easy to take those Ulster-Scot families that I had come to know so well and trace them back to their precise origins in Scotland. It would just be a question, presumably, of finding out the names of the ordinary men and women who had left Scotland and come over to Ulster; the exact places they had come from; and when.

Working on those premises I started the search in January 1985 and consulted the appropriate authorities in Edinburgh; the Scottish Genealogy Society; the Scots Ancestry Research Council; the Scottish Register Office;

the Scottish Record Office; the National Library of Scotland; the separate but admirable National Library Map Department out at Causewayside; and other offices and libraries there. But to little or no avail. Apart from turning up a few original seventeenth century manuscripts in the Record Office I was surprised to come across no worked material relevant to my quest; and even more surprised to find little knowledge of the problem and little or no interest. Indeed I sensed indifference in Edinburgh.

The staff at the splendid Mitchell Library in Glasgow proved to be more understanding and sympathetic. So also did Librarians and Curators at Irvine, Ayr, Kilmarnock, Stranraer, Wigtown, Kirkcudbright, Dumfries, Hawick, Jedburgh, Melrose, Selkirk, Peebles, Biggar and Carlisle. Intensive study led to my looking at some two hundred local histories and some ten thousand family names recorded over the centuries. But still nothing relevant to my quest appeared.

Realising that I was working on my own and to some extent in the dark I then thought it sensible to seek help from others. I wrote to (or consulted in person) about twenty local history societies in the south of Scotland. I specially consulted the organisations responsible for the graves and memorials of the persecuted seventeenth century covenanters. I advertised in magazines and submitted letters to newspapers. I calculated the spread of names in graveyard inscriptions, newspaper notices, street directories, telephone books and electoral rolls; and sent off letters to unsuspecting residents with likely names and addresses. Taking my courage in my hands I importuned up to a dozen university dons (only to hear a lot about the university 'cuts').

Gradually it was becoming clear that I was ploughing new ground; that this subject had never been researched; that there was no published or unpublished work on my subject; and that there was indeed no interest in the subject in Scotland. When, for example, I asked the Curator of the Museum in Dumfries about the Scottish side to the story of Scottish migration to Ulster he responded crisply, cruelly but honestly: 'What you seek does not exist'. Plain talk (though I took some quiet amusement from noticing that the approach to his Museum (and wonderful 'camera obscura') is through a street called 'Ulster Place').

Much has been written, in other words, on Anglo-Scottish affairs in the seventeenth century and much also on Anglo-Irish affairs; but precious little work has been done on Scottish-Irish affairs at that time. And what work has been done has been almost entirely done, as far as I can see, from the Ulster side. As well as the classic works by the Rev. George Hill a hundred years ago and by Professor Theo Moody in the 1930s, we have Dr David Stevenson's long and careful study of the 1640 wars *'Scottish Covenanters and Irish Confederates'* in 1981; and now in 1985 Dr Raymond Gillespie's academic work *'Colonial Ulster'*.

But in my judgement, for what it is worth, head and shoulders above them all stands Michael Perceval-Maxwell's great work *'The Scottish Migration to Ulster in the Reign of James I'*, published in 1973 so far as relevance to the social, economic and human problems of the Ulster-Scot origins is concerned.

Perceval-Maxwell covers exactly the ground that those few of us concerned with the problem of the human and personal aspect of the Scottish migration wish to see covered; and in doing so he of course uses modern material and up-to-date methods of social and economic analysis. But even he stops tantalizingly short of helping the genealogist. At page xii of his Preface he writes: 'In a study of this nature it is all too easy to sink into a morass of names . . . indeed I have tried to keep the number of names in the text to a minimum'. And yet it is precisely names that some of us would have wished him to supply. I have corresponded with him in Montreal on the point. I have also corresponded with Dr Gillespie in Dublin for he comes even closer to our problem in a detailed painstaking map of name distribution in Scotland.

To be clear, the general history of the movement from Scotland to Ulster has been studied and written up by those historians as well as the decisions and actions of the Kings and the parts played by the top people, the generals and the gentry. What I have been struggling to do is to get one step further down the social ladder and to identify the ordinary men and women, the farmers, tradesmen and others who actually formed the Migration and who in practical terms ploughed the land and built the farmhouses in Aughanloo and the Roe Valley in those pioneering days — in other words, the forefathers of many of us.

EVIDENCE

Documentary evidence has been hard to come by. This is not because Scottish records are poor. A great deal of documentation has survived from the seventeenth and even the sixteenth century in Scotland. After two years of intensive work I regard the records as being plentiful and as having been extremely well kept — not quite so comprehensive as in England but vastly more so than in Ireland, for obvious reasons. On my particular subject I could trace the famous men like Sir Robert McLellan of Bombie, Kirkcudbright and James Haig of Bemersyde, Melrose, who were granted large tracts of land by the King (but who took precious little interest personally in the practical problems, so far as I can see). I can also trace some of the Lairds to whom the harder tasks of settlement were assigned. King James sensibly favoured the rural Lairds over the city merchants for these responsibilities in Ulster, partly because they were better able to defend themselves and their properties but partly also — and I find this most significant — because they were less grasping, less anxious for a quick profit.

But it is the next layer down which I was looking for, the farmers and the tradesmen who came over to County Londonderry, ploughed the land, sowed the seed, reaped the harvest and to a large extent fed the population in those times, according to the Pynnar Survey Report of 1619. The well-known and I suppose universal problem of the absence of humble people from the history books was further compounded in my search by three additional factors stressed to me by my friend Mr Alf Truckell of Carsethorn, Kirkbean, doyen of local historians in Dumfries and Galloway. First, rural dwellers came to notice a great deal less than town dwellers. Second, farm tenants had a sensible practice of deputing one of their number to travel to the Laird's castle and pay all their rents together, with the result that many a real, faithful rent-paying tenant simply did not appear on the Laird's working rent roll. Third, law-abiding people came to notice a lot less often than law-breakers and so did not adorn the pages of those interminable Court Proceedings that abound in early Scottish records.

It was of course obvious to me that as I was examining turbulent events in far-off times the likelihood of finding attested personal records or neat shipping lists was negligible. Negligible but not altogether out of the question. The migration under King James I, far from being the disorderly flight of a rabble, was in fact a planned operation involving designated zones, authorized ports, certificates of denization and in the end passports, specimen signatures and much necessary and sensible red tape.

As the result of some two hundred approaches which I have made by letter, telephone or personal visit I am satisfied that it should be just about possible to trace some of the ordinary emigrants, even though I personally failed to do so in any satisfactory and reliable way. All that being so, I decided to devise a number of other approaches to see whether they might help. My first thought was for tracing some lines of migration on the strength of dialect. Here I followed the splendid linguistic maps (covering Scotland and Ulster) of J.Y. Mather and thought I could discern direct similarities between Kintyre and The Route, Ayrshire and mid-Antrim, Galloway and Magilligan; but there were so many overlaps and discrepancies that I made up my mind that I could not draw any safe conclusions. I greatly regretted that failure as I believe that dialect has been shown to provide useful clues in other areas such as the emigration of peoples from Europe to North America.

I then tried ethnic breads in an effort at tracing some precise lines of migration from a common predilection for soda bread, wheaten farls, potato oaten, pot-oven scones and so on. But this produced nothing but reflections of the obvious. Next I looked at house-types and early methods of building to see whether it might be possible to identify similarities between one area in Scotland and one in County Londonderry. Unfortunately my understanding of the subject did not reach far enough. In the same sense I thought, and I still think, that a study of folk music and folk song, legends, sayings and proverbs might serve to trace some lines of popular migration; but again my own limitations ruled out any more profitable study.

The migration — not just the organized Plantation under King James but also the Hamilton and Montgomery settlement of 1601–1610, the New Scots Army of the 1640s and the flight of the harassed covenanters in later years — was by any standard a sizeable event, causing possibly fifty thousand to a hundred thousand men, women and children to leave their homes, their friends and neighbours in Scotland (out of a total Scottish population of half a million to possibly a million). It is a matter of continuing surprise to me that such a migration should have left no trace whatever in the from of letters, stories, poems, street ballads or other folk material. And yet I am assured by Scottish authorities that that is the fact of the matter. Perhaps I might interpose here that I have tried to deal with that and many other human aspects of the whole problem in much greater detail in a lengthy work entitled: *'GIRL — NAME FORGOTTEN . . .'* deposited in typescript in Public Record Offices.

The suggestion was put to me informally from the National Library of Scotland that in seeking evidence of origins *in* Scotland I was starting from the wrong end. I ought instead to establish all about my people from early seventeenth century documents in Ulster and only then try to trace the threads back to Scotland. That of course was totally out of the question because of the well-known state of Irish records resulting from certain historical events. Another practical suggestion, this time from Belfast, was to work in exactly the opposite direction, namely to make 'an intelligent guess' about likely origins in Scotland, that is to say to assume that our people came through the harbour to say Irvine or Ayr or Portpatrick and then concentrate on a thorough search of that area. But I could make equally little of that idea, either.

Heraldry was a long shot that I thought might just possibly reveal or suggest some lines of descent and therefore of movement; but to little purpose, again. I did establish one Oliver motto that appeared consistently (in a context I shall be describing in a moment): 'Ad Foedera Cresco', and have decided to hold it as a marker but I have not been able to develop that matter.

METHODOLOGY

The method I finally adopted was as follows and, for better or for worse, it is entirely my own. I plotted laboriously the areas in southern Scotland where our family and neighbourhood names predominated before and after 1600; and then tried to see where that led. I think I can claim that this is at any rate a promising line to follow. Oliver, not on the surface the most Scottish sounding name, you might think, turned out to be easy. The name abounds in *one* area — Hawick, Melrose, Kelso, Jedburgh, Denholm, Jedforest and away up to those bleak moors on the English border at Carter Bar — let us say for convenience Jedburgh and ten miles around (which is the way I like to see these questions in terms of human beings, farming and understandable commercial activity).

There I found Olivers in large numbers and in high profile from 1200 onwards, cropping up (and influencing the area) as farmers, lawyers, Crusaders, soldiers, cavalrymen, horse thieves, smugglers, town clerks, football players, raiders, reivers (an important title in those debatable lands), parsons, bankers, pie-makers, auctioneers, and much else. The Christian names (our Christian names in Ulster also) of John, Andrew, James and George predominate.

In Monipenny's List of Border Clans in 1603 there is actually an Oliver Clan with no fewer than three members cited as chieftains (not a healthy sign, I fear, for it suggests that there was no agreement on a Chief, which probably explains why Olivers did not survive as a Clan but only as a 'surname' in Border terminology).

With such a huge concentration of Olivers in Jedforest (and I have confirmed it from many angles on the spot) the question is not where did the Olivers come from but where did they go to? Some of them moved down as the result partly of overcrowding, partly of adventure and partly of unhappy conflict with the law, to Liddesdale and Langholm (north of Carlisle) and then on, I think, to the fertile lands and prosperous seaports of Dumfries and Kirkcudbright where I have personally found many firm and interesting references to Olivers and especially to John Olivers. To me those references tie in well, in style, character and associations, with the Olivers of The Borders on the one hand and with the Olivers of north Derry on the other hand. I have developed those links much more fully in *'GIRL — NAME FORGOTTEN . . .'*

Of all those references the most relevant is the authentic individual case in 1618 of John Oliver of Billies in Kelton near Kirkcudbright town, living close to the minor lairds who leased Lord Kirkcudbright's lands from him around (but not in) Limavady. I am glad to have been able to perform a small service to other researchers by pin-pointing with National Grid References, to six digits, the exact places from which those minor lairds came as well as the townlands around Limavady to which they went — for the first time ever.

This John Oliver is clearly recorded in the detailed and readable Records of the 'Burrow' of Kirkcudbright as incurring a loan of twenty-two pounds in 1618 from a man called Mickle; his nearest neighbour was Edward Forrest or Forrester. Both Mickle and Forrest took some of those leases in North Derry. John Oliver would obviously have known all about their good fortune (for he lived just across the field from them as I have established by walking over the land) and would either have been recruited by them (along with his brother James) or would have pushed himself forward as a volunteer. In either event a loan of twenty-two pounds would have come in handy for buying a horse and a plough and for paying the charges, the exorbitant charges, being asked for the sea passage from Kirkcudbright to Coleraine.

In so far as those suppositions hold good we can now see a credible line of descent from John Oliver, Prepositus of Berwick in the 13th century down through the prolific if notorious Olivers of Jedforest and their outliers in Dumfries and Kirkcudbright, across the sea to the early settlers around Limavady and then on down to the present day. In that putative sense the youngest Olivers and their siblings of today can look back on something like twenty-five generations of ancestors in a recognizable pattern of nominal, social, economic, administrative and religious life.

Of course that line of descent lacks an enormous amount in firmness and documentation. But as I have come across no other pattern that offers any probability nearly as strong as that one, we may adopt it as the best working hypothesis we have. And it can be sustained also for several of the long-standing friends and neighbours notably Douglas, Shannon, Connell, Trotter, Irwin and the others equally close in Galloway and in Derry.

The Sherrards or Shearers of earlier times predominate in mid-Ayrshire. Going on my own detailed calculations I place their homeland around Ayr, Irvine and Kilmarnock and I have walked over much of it. I have not followed up the second homeland of the Shearers given by G.F. Black as the north-east coast running up from Dundee to Aberdeen — for two reasons. First I could trace no grant of land in County Londonderry to Undertakers from that region; second I could see neither in G.F. Black's Dictionary nor in Sir Iain Moncreiffe's wonderful map ('Clan Map, Scotland of Old', prepared by Sir Iain Moncrieffe of that Ilk and Don Pottinger, Herald of Arms. Bartholemew & Son. Edinburgh.) any sign of other Magilligan names whereas Ayrshire is rich in Allison, Morrison, McCracken and so on. Some of those Ayrshire Shearers could well have migrated with any of the great movements in the seventeenth century but I have no knowledge of that nor any pointers to persons and places.

A more likely course was a more circuitous one. In the middle of the sixteenth century many Protestants were driven out of Ayrshire and over to Bute and the Kintyre peninsula. Then around 1600 or so the McDonnell powers encouraged them to move further and indeed just across the few miles of sea to north Antrim. I have always been struck, from my own observation, by the close similarity of the dialect in that 'Route' area with the dialect of

Magilligan (skipping Coleraine). My assumption therefore is that these Protestant Ayrshire refugees through Bute and Kintyre settled first in The Route in the last years of the sixteenth century and moved over into County Londonderry when that area was being opened up under King James I. Sistrakeel and Drumraighland (mentioned above as being for long the authenticated home of the Shearers) lay in the 'take' or 'Proportion' of the Company of Fishmongers. The Company found it hard, impossible indeed, to hold their ill-prepared and ill-suited English settlers who quickly became disenchanted with living conditions. That being so, the Fishmongers would quite naturally have looked for reliable replacements in the persons of durable Scots farmers. And, in those circumstances, the Shearers (and Allisons, Lintons, Morrisons, McCrackens) — refugees twice over, remember — would have been glad to take up tenancies in that rather unattractive, hilly land above Ballykelly. Then (as I have shown earlier) they moved down around 1750–1780 to the pleasanter life on the salubrious Magilligan plain and the more easily worked sandy soil there.

The Rev George Hill takes us even further back than the 1600 date I have been working on, for he dates the first arrivals from Bute (next to Kintyre) at 1560 (the Archibald Stewarts of Ballintoy). The Shearers, Conns, Allisons, Morrisons, Lintons, McCrackens and other eventual Magilligan settlers could well have come over after the Stewarts and could therefore conceivably be amongst the earliest Scottish settlers in modern Ulster. Once again that line of descent lacks an enormous amount in firmness; but in other aspects it has the ring of truth about it. And I know of no other more convincing one.

Support for those hypotheses of mine concerning Oliver and Sherrard and their friends and neighbours on both sides of the sea comes from the acknowledged authority on names in the south of Scotland, my good friend Robert Shannon of Eastriggs and Dumfries who has compiled and plotted (on charts and maps) a truly monumental index of names, places and dates. He sees much to support my suppositions and patterns and nothing to contradict them. I was happy, just before Robert Archibald Shannon died in March 1987, to show him that if John Oliver migrated to north Derry around 1618, so also did a Robert Shannon who appeared with the Olivers in the authentic Limavady Muster Rolls of 1630 or earlier. The Shannons continued to live next door to the Douglas's and the Olivers at Derrybeg right into the twentieth century.

PART IV

More work to be done

The efforts related above show that some patterns of movement by untitled and unpropertied people from the south of Scotland to the north of Ireland in the seventeenth century can fairly be presumed and sketched; but they show even more clearly that the task of tracing the individuals concerned is extremely difficult. Difficult but not impossible. There are one or two encouraging signs.

One of the many new friends I have made in this search — a McCracken from Portpatrick — has told me that she recalls her father, a Minister of the Kirk there, often talking at their fireside of the McCracken relatives they had in Ulster over the centuries. And what name has for so long been so redolent of the Magilligan plain as McCracken? Again, and much more impressively, the McBroom family of Holestone-Doagh can positively and with documentation trace their descent back to the McBrooms featured in the Records of Kirkcudbright in the late 1500s and early 1600s. I also know that Elma Wickens of Bangor has, by her own untiring efforts and considerable skill, traced one branch of her family back firmly to John Irwin, Convenor of Trades in Dumfries at the beginning of the eighteenth century. Moreover Professor Perceval-Maxwell has not ruled out to me the eventual possibility of further individual and family connections being traced.

Again I have been impressed in this connection by some learned papers I have just seen by Professor R.J. Gregg, formerly of Larne and of Queen's University Belfast. This remarkable phonetician has traced at least one vowel-sound back from the Gleno Valley to Tarbolton in Ayrshire, exactly the sort of thing I was trying to do in my amateur fashion. What is more, Professor Gregg has written in 'ORBIS: Bulletin International de Documentation Linguistique', page 392: 'A detailed investigation of these Scotch-Irish dialects — which would be of considerable value to dialectologists not only in the British Isles but probably also in English-speaking North America — still remains to be carried out'. Exactly my point. And of course Professor Braidwood of Queens had been hard at work in that field as well.

My submission is that the quest for precise Scottish origins is well worth pursuing. The Ulster-Scot heritage deserves at least as much from us. Considering the amount of public money and time spent over the last twenty-five years or so in promoting the Ulster-Scot tradition in America, it is surprising that the bodies concerned should have done nothing, apparently, to further the Scottish connection and nothing, it seems, to engage the interest and collaboration of the authorities in Scotland. Would this not also have been a suitable and worthy task for the scholars of the Presbyterian Church in terms of the named individuals who made up the early Church? Existing Church histories make disappointing reading if one is looking for the human values of the ordinary men and women who migrated and filled the pews in the new churches.

Although I have been suggesting for the past year or two that the quest I have sketched might form the basis for a joint study promoted either by Queens or the University of Ulster and either Glasgow or Strathclyde University, no historian there has shown any interest. Only the Institute of Irish Studies in Queens University has. A more effective programme of relevant research might be mounted as a joint effort under the direction of the PRONI and the Ulster Folk and Transport Museum in collaboration with their opposite numbers in Scotland. A joint professional team could obviously achieve vastly more in documentary research than I have been able to do. And such a team, with specialist advisers, would also be admirably suited to researching the many other aspects — dialect, transport, house-types, folklore, music, ballads, sayings and the other features of popular culture that underlie much of our heritage.

If those ideas seem far-fetched or over-ambitious let me say bluntly that many Scots today look on *our* Ulster-Scot pioneers of Empire and the New World (including those Presidents of the USA) as simply Scotsmen who travelled abroad by way of the north of Ireland and used our harbours as

convenient ports of embarkation. This does little to support those Ulster-
American homesteads and parks which we lovingly promote in the north of
Ireland.

All that I have been saying here is important but not by any means all-
important and it is salutary, in this as in life generally, to keep a sense of
balance. To that end I finish now by repeating some words which I used in
winding off a series of popular articles published by the Northern Constitution
at Coleraine in February 1986:

'The widespread indifference which I found in Scotland [to the Scottish
Migration to Ulster under the Scottish King James VI and I] may help a little
to restore some balance in the perception of history. Whereas many look on
the seventeenth century migration as one of the biggest events in history (for
better or for worse) that event is seen through Scottish eyes as just one short
phase in the long story of the ebb and flow of peoples across the sea.'

On Having an English Mother-in-law

From the 'front' of the Cave Hill, that is to say the table-top summit that faces south and east you get a stunning view – to Belfast Lough and on out to the Irish Sea, to the low wooded Holywood Hills, to the soft green Castlereagh Hills, up the Lagan Valley, along to the big heights of Divis, the Black Mountain and Collin – and cradled in the embrace of this wide circle, the City of Belfast itself.

To the North and West the scene is very different. The table-top tilts 'back' over the moorland of the great basalt mass that starts just there. With that aspect the 'back' of the Cave Hill gets less sun and more wind and is in every way much bleaker.

Yet that was the spot chosen by Muriel for a family picnic on Boxing Day 1942 and where she produced her all-too-recognizable sandwiches of rough brown bread filled with, literally, cold boiled cabbage. My first introduction.

Muriel Lucy Fox, married to Howell Ritson, was the most unusual person I have ever known on personal and intimate terms; and I owe a great deal to her.

Her vegetarianism must be mentioned first, her extreme, intense, uncompromising aversion to animal flesh – meat, ham, fowl and fish – and her strenuous promotion of a diet of fruit, vegetables, bread, cereals, nuts, raisins and herbs. She came close to veganism – which eschews eggs, milk and milk products as well – but stopped short of full conversion. She stood close also to Nature Cure. Her views sprang from several sources – ethical, aesthetic – have you ever actually stood in a working abattoir? – medical, economic – how much more efficient to grow vegetables and fruit to eat than to grow cereals for feeding animals to be slaughtered eventually for human food – and, finally, spiritual.

But it was the intensity of her feelings that impressed everyone, the utter rejection of white bread, dried egg, rennet puddings and so on, not only in ardent principle but in stringent, vigorous daily practice as well.

Muriel and Howell were pioneers in vegetarianism and food reform away back in the 1920s. They had of course many distinguished models – Gandhi and George Bernard Shaw, for example, not to mention Hitler and Mussolini; and the impact they made on Ulster when they moved there in 1942 was striking. Here was, after all, an essentially rural community; every Belfast man was said to have still 'the glaur of the countryside on his heels'; the few vegetarians that struggled to keep the faith (on an enforced diet of endless omelettes) were of course looked on as freaks. By the time Muriel left Ulster the vegetarian community was strong and expanding; it was no longer just an eccentric clique; by the 1980s vegetarianism was fully established as an acceptable way of life and of restaurant catering, even if still a bit of a puzzle to many.

Muriel converted to Quakerism in her early married years and again pursued the faith and practice with courage, energy and persistence. There

47

had been a Quaker Movement in Ulster for hundreds of years, in Belfast, Lisburn, Lurgan, Armagh and that line of English settlement along the Lagan Valley into mid-Ulster. To Muriel it seemed old-fashioned, evangelical and none too 'sound' on the all-important Peace Testimony. It was here that I came to appreciate the enormously practical, active, courageous side of her Quakerism. When for example Jack and Kathe Shemeld needed to get away from the cares of running one of the boarding houses at Friends School Lisburn, under John and Norah Douglas the legendary Heads, it was Muriel who without hesitation stepped in and took responsibility for running the house – caring for the carers, as we would say to-day. And still more practical and helpful perhaps was the knack she had for cajoling unsuspecting young people to lend a hand in her various human enterprises; one for example was a lovely girl from County Cork, the now famous cook and caterer, Myrtle Allen. Or again, when a young Quaker mother in Cherryvalley took seriously ill and other people spoke kind words or helped for an hour or two, Muriel took the young baby into her house and accepted full responsibility for it. This was nothing new for her. She had all her adult life befriended worried people and taken them under her wing in her own home.

When Howell died suddenly from a heart attack in 1948 and a funeral ceremony was being held in the packed Meeting House in Frederick Street, Muriel, despite her evident distress and grief, stood up, addressed the Meeting for Worship and in a few straight, clear, bold sentences conveyed the message from her dear husband: Whatever you undertake to do, do it with all your heart and all your strength. It was a remarkable feat. People quoted these words over and over again in Belfast for years to come. In many ways courage is the greatest virtue.

Anti-vivisection ran alongside her vegetarianism and Quakerism. So did anti-vaccination. And so did Rights of Way (a lot less needed in Ulster than in England). More important and more valuable was her spirited advocacy of soil protection and soil purity and what we would call 'organic' culture to-day. Here again she was – we now can see – well ahead of her time.

Far from being treated as solitary pursuits, all those causes were driven forward in a white heat of meetings, consultations, telephone calls, cabals and, above all, letter-writing. Muriel was a prodigious letter-writer; and a prodigious sender-on of letters. She thought it wrong and wasteful to throw into a drawer some interesting letter she had received from a Professor of Soil Chemistry or a working gardener or a Weighty Quaker or a Headmaster or a poor half-literate woman with whom she had once upon a time shared rooms. Her own letters – in a loose sort of untidy scrawl – would reach you in a package of letters passed on from other people – whether they knew or not and whether they consented or not. That was one of the ways in which she kept alive an enormous network of collaborators in her many radiant causes.

Exceptional energy, both physical and mental, kept her flame burning brightly. She was for example a gardener of unusual intensity. When we went to stay with her – (often in some chilly cottage well above the snow-line) and came straggling down to breakfast at eight or half past eight, Muriel had already completed two hours' work in her garden – or in that of a neighbour who needed help. (Even in her Seventies and Eighties she would insist on doing work for 'the old people' as she described her younger friends). Breakfast was a treat, with hunks of home-baked bread already toasted for us at the fire, heaps of nuts, raisins and fruit loosely piled up on the table and a pottery jar of her own delicious 'potted stuff', a blend of margarine, Marmite and herbs. One underlying aspect of this performance was hard to take: Muriel would deliberately start her day early, deliberately have breakfast ready, ostentatiously stand about waiting for us with the unspoken intention of showing us up as laggards or as she herself would have put it: 'heaping coals of fire on your heads'.

Muriel Fox was very English in every way, without a trace or suggestion of Celtic or other strain in her make-up. English by descent; the daughter of a Church of England clergyman (at Martindale away up in the Lake District Fells, the highest parish in England); educated at a very English Boarding School (Sidcot in Somerset, where she had been Head Girl around 1908). It is true to say that although she impinged on the Ulster and the Irish scene at many points, and with some considerable impact, she never really connected with the local people in spirit or in the sense of civic and business affairs. The cultural gap was too wide and coming over at the age of fifty-two she would have had a problem in trying to adjust. But, still, she faced the gap and tackled the problem in her own unique way as I have tried to show.

And yet the dimensions of her range of interests were a constant surprise. Few people in Ulster did more to welcome refugees from Central Europe, amongst whom she made life-long friends and acquired devoted admirers.

Such a personality has of course many different sides. One surprise for example was to find that – underneath all those burning convictions and fearsome practices – there lay an earthy sense of humour. One of her funniest stories concerned her meeting a young, dark-haired Mother on the village street, stopping to admire the red-haired baby in the pram and asking helpfully whether the Father had red hair too. Muriel would insist with glee that the Mother replied: 'I have no idea. He never took his hat off'. Whether it was the suddenness of the encounter, the brevity of the friendship or the sheer skill in keeping on his hat (not a cap, notice) throughout the embrace that impressed Muriel we never knew.

As a native Ulsterman with all my beliefs, prejudices and convictions I had a big problem in relating to my Mother-in-law. While I admired her and liked her I found the intensity hard to live with in the midst of my own busy life and conflicting duties to our children; and some of her attitudes plainly wrong and dangerous – as for example the rejection of vaccination against small-pox, then still a public health hazard because of war-time migration and huge troop movements in and out of Ulster. My response in the early years, for better or for worse, was to carry on every normal aspect of family life and relationship and above all to encourage our five boys to benefit from her company and her extraordinary stimulus, but for my own part to keep just a small polite distance between us. I could see that if I did not, then Muriel would have quickly taken me over body and soul. And after all a man is surely entitled to eat a slice of white bread now and again, is he not?

Muriel's overpowering force of will and influence must be counted one of several reasons why I never joined the Society of Friends even though I supported them in many ways. To me the Society appeared as an ethical club rather than a theological church and as such was attractive to me. But my acute sense of independence – my Ulster stubbornness if you will – prevented me from surrendering to an embrace that would have totally smothered me. So I stuck to my Ulster-Scot Presbyterianism.

Still, energy in a person is a powerful attraction and as the years went on I grew closer and closer to Muriel. As the intensity of her purpose waned with age and maturity and as mine waxed with experience and confidence, our two levels of feeling and understanding came to equal one another. In the end, in her final years when she was approaching ninety, I found I was closer to Muriel Lucy Fox Ritson than anyone else was.

On Saying Good-bye to Unionism
and Nationalism

Let the first sentence of the first paragraph of this Essay express the greatest need in the whole Irish situation: the need for Ulster's position as an integral part of the United Kingdom to be stated beyond yea or nay, enacted at Westminster, recorded at the United Nations and made clear to everyone.

Ministers will of course say that that already is the position. Few people in Ulster believe them.

How could they? How could they believe that the constitutional position was secure when the same Ministers on another day legislate for a Referendum on the Border; when they say that Irish Unification is a legitimate aim; when the first aim of Ulster Nationalists goes straight for unification with the Republic; and when well-meaning but ill-informed political parties in London still talk so foolishly of "unification by consent", dangerously stirring the explosive pot.

How could anyone believe that the position was secure so long as the Eire Constitution of 1937 claims jurisdiction over the North and so long as Britain falls in with that outrageous claim? Silence in that serious situation can surely be read as meaning consent or at any rate acquiescence. How could anyone believe the position was firm and secure so long as the Dublin Court Ruling holds that those Articles amount not just to a hope but to a "constitutional imperative"?

One of the many reasonable objections to the disastrous Anglo–Irish Agreement of 1985 was that the same document could be read two ways: by some, as underlining Ulster's position in the United Kingdom and by others as confirming Articles 2 and 3. What a mess.

And in their haste, their impatience, to foster the uncertainty, H.M.Government in the very first Article of that regrettable document pledged their readiness to promote legislation for Irish Unification if required.

All those doubts and ambiguities about the most fundamental question in all politics: "What is your country?" are keenly felt in Ulster and are responsible for much of the present tragedy.

They lie at the heart of the Unionist problem. However much you may find Unionist spokesmen unattractive and disagree with their tactics and deplore their rhetoric, you must see the crippling weakness of their basic situation and the disabling effect it is bound to have on them.

That is the reason why Unionism has always seemed so negative, why Unionists appear to be always saying "No", always on the defensive, clinging to slogans such as "No Surrender" and "Not an Inch".

They have always felt under threat. Is it any wonder that they run to their laager for safety?

That sense of insecurity – paranoid as it must seem to outsiders – is heightened immeasurably by the way in which every action by

H.M.Government in relation to the Irish Republic has to be viewed in Ulster against that backcloth of uncertainty. The combination of the Government's obsession with placating Dublin and the ambiguity of their attitude to the North's position leads unionists at every level to read far too much into small actions that are no doubt harmless, possibly even beneficial, in themselves but which are so readily seen in Ballymena or Lisburn as "selling us down the river." In their own interests, if for no other reasons, H.M.Government would be wise to remove all possible ground for suspicion and so evoke a more positive attitude from their own citizens in the North.

Times are changing.

The desire of the Irish Republic to take over the North has disappeared. Ordinary citizens in the Republic have not for some time had any real interest in taking over "The Black North", and now-a-days, after twenty-five years of disorder and violence they would run a mile at the very prospect of managing and paying for the North. For my own part in the course of years of digging into family history over the centuries I conclude that the Southerners look on the North as another country, on Newry as a frontier town and on Ulstermen as awkward and thrawn. One election campaign in the Republic after another has shown how little the people are concerned. Few know the North. Few ever go there. Yet, all the while, Southern politicians have felt obliged to make ritual references on formal occasions to "our people in the North" – quite the most sectarian stance in the whole Irish situation. Such rituals are far removed from the concerns of ordinary men and women in Dundalk or Drogheda.

Times are changing in Dublin politics, too. There is a noticeable cooling-off in Republican rhetoric and much more concern with their own domestic problems. Unification of Ireland has sunk far down the Agenda of Southern parties – for the time being, at any rate.

The Irish Taoiseach himself is said to believe that any thought of Irish Unity has been put back for a generation or so and even that is no doubt a statesmanlike underestimate. Such a telling assessment ought to be built upon and used to good purpose. Why encourage uncertainty and instability where none need exist now? Let us go all out for stability.

And it has dropped down the current Agenda of the Ulster Social Democratic and Labour Party – for the time being, too. They are now heard talking less about Unification and more of joint bodies and Condominium. This is not the time to analyse the practical horrors of Condominium but merely to say that it would in practice be unworkable if the present constitutional uncertainty were to persist. It would not be Condominium but Contradominium.

Free of any personal responsibility now, I can take the liberty of using an informal essay to put up an idea that is at once simple and yet far-reaching and beneficial to all but irredentist militant republicans.

The best single step in the whole situation would be if H.M.Government, after open, quick consultation with all interested parties, were to legislate for Northern Ireland to be and to remain for, say, fifty years a part of the United Kingdom state with no ifs and buts, no quibbling, full stop. And to do so at once.

I am speaking here of the state in the strictest philosophical sense, the self-contained and self-sufficient entity based on the rational authority of its unity and offering all its citizens equal rights and duties. What I am saying does

little more than follow the teachings of Hegel, the great political and philosophical thinker some two hundred years ago, when he distinguished between
state and society and defined the affairs of state in terms of rights not of race.
I am not speaking of society nor for one moment suggesting that Ulster
Republicans and Nationalists should be expected to join some sort of polite
English cultural club. They would be free to practise their own distincitve
culture, language and customs within the diverse multi-cultural system now
obviously developing throughout the United Kingdom.

Much good could flow.

Unionists, whether with a big U or a small u, would be re-assured for the
first time ever and could relax with honour and dignity, secure in the knowledge
that they had achieved their aim at last. At the same time existing Nationalists
would gain in even greater measure by being freed at a stroke from their
prolonged disadvantage of being a permanent minority. And it is well to recall
that they have more in common with their Northern neighbours than they
have with their Southern sympathizers. I doubt whether many in their heart
of hearts, after a public protest, would shed a tear over finding themselves
firmly and clearly within the United Kingdom assured of certainty, stability
and social and economic progress. Deep down I believe that their greatest
desire is for equal status, for an end to second-class citizenship as they see it;
a desire more likely to be guaranteed within the United Kingdom than in any
other setting. And by the same process Sinn Fein and the IRA would be given
the most telling answer to their campaign.

I would set up, under the new Act and for all forms of local election, a
statutory Electoral Register of political parties in Ulster, to which new parties
would be invited to subscribe, with new names, new aims related to the future
not to the past, accepting the Constitution, giving clear support to all the
institutions of the State and forswearing political violence in every shape and
form.

I would then withdraw recognition from all existing parties, and let a fresh
start be made. All politicians would be forced to think anew.

The terms"Unionism" and "Nationalism" would disappear because they
would have no relevance to the facts.

There would be another great gain.

One of the baffling paradoxes of Ulster is the gulf that has existed since
1921 (and has increased enormously in the last twenty years) between the
political stage on the one hand – crippled by constitutional instability and
enforced negativism – and on the other hand the world of business, trade
unions, the professions, the schools and colleges, the health service, the civil
and public service corps, the arts, the enormous growth of vigorous voluntary
bodies bursting with ability, energy and imagination. Immediate headway
would be made if the two could be brought closer together with the return to
public life and politics of every hue of all these men and women who have
withdrawn to the golf courses, the yacht clubs and the more expensive
restaurants. No single step could do more to bring about that switch than the
steps I am urging here in this Essay.

There lies a true task of statesmanship to-day, to bring to bear on democratic
politics the full weight of talent amongst Ulster's men and women, instead of
wearily negotiating the minutiae of where and precisely how to bring to the
negotiating table committed and entrenched political parties that are

irreconcilably opposed to one another on fundamental questions of the very constitution itself – with all the distrust that those questions inevitably breed.

What new parties would emerge is impossible to foresee. Certainly all those faithful supporters of the Alliance Party would have a flying start and would feel rewarded after twenty years of patient work. Those who man the present Nationalist camp could easily be seen helping to run the Province with their proven ability and eloquence, provided they fully and effectively shed their image as the Trojan Horse. I hate saying so, but that has always been very close to the heart of the whole matter. Or the way would then be open for all the main British parties to campaign, regardless of religious affiliations. Or a Business Party. Or an Agrarian Party. Or a Social Policy Party or whatever people wanted to have.

To be clear I am not suggesting that removing constitutional ambiguity should necessarily result in total absorption into the London legal and administrative system. That would be one option but only one. Legislative and administrative devolution is another option – and the one which I favour. And there is the simpler option of ceasing to waste time looking for an "solution" and, instead, treating legislation and administration for Northern Ireland on the same footing as Scotland or Wales. And there could well be many variants to meet the feelings of local people – so long as all doubt about the basic constitution were firmly ruled out, with every elected politician pledged to uphold the constitution of his country – surely a fair and reasonable condition after so much bloodshed and misery. To be clear again I am far from suggesting that a firm declaration would be the end of the road. It would just be the start of a number of new roads. There could well be closer relations with the Republic under European rules on a basis of equality, absence of threat and mutual respect. With vision a lead could actually be given to a movement, in step with Scotland, Wales and Northern England towards thoroughgoing, regional government, diversity within unity. With foresight it is even possible to look ahead to greater regional government within the new European Community, "l'Europe à cent drapeaux". That is where new thinking could be most exciting.

I am simply talking here of confirming the boundaries of the United Kingdom. Hardly a revolutionary idea? There are of course subtleties of argument and shades of sensitive feeling but they add up merely to tiresome word-spinning seen against stagnation, despair and violence for the rest of our days.

This proposal of mine is no new idea. I developed it as long ago as 1988 when I wrote a comprehensive Article in *"The Political Quarterly"*, Volume 59 No.4.

Direct Rule has done much good for Ulster through the exercise of those great British virtues – pragmatism, hardwork and steadfast administration. But, given all its power, influence and money, it has not noticeably raised the condition of ordinary people; and some competent observers find that society is more divided now than at any time for generations past. Direct Rule has achieved absolutely nothing to release Ulster politics from the crushing straight-jacket of unionism versus nationalism. If anything, it has strength-ened that sterile conflict by its close association with the Irish Republic. An injection of what Britain (and more especially England) lacks – imagination – would be a great help. I should like to see the BBC in Ulster (as well as the independent publicity agencies) take on a duty to recruit new thinkers to promote a vigorous campaign for politics aimed at the real needs of people and benefitting the many sectors of what is now, sadly, a fragmented society of able and energetic men and women. The people have suffered too much, the citizens in the rest of the United Kingdom have been too indifferent about the boundaries of their own realm, the views from outside have been too simplistic; the so-called "solutions" have been too convoluted. Simpler, bolder steps than might be contemplated in Great Britain to-day would be amply justified here by the facts of the human condition before our very eyes. Let us go to it and say good-bye to the past of Ulster politics.

POSTSCRIPT

This essay was written in 1993 and flowed from the more fully reasoned analysis in "*The Political Quarterly*" of 1988. Both were composed in times that were uncommonly dangerous and murderous for Ulster and Britain. I considered both pieces to be timely, helpful and above all stimulating in those circumstances.

The IRA cease-fire of 31st August 1994 has created a new situation (holding much promise but also many uncertainties) in which any unilateral declaration by Britain would be out of place. Nevertheless this essay has within it several ideas which readers may find worthwhile: the hope of getting away from the sterile opposition of unionism and nationalism; the case for new political parties; the urgent need to bring back into public life the many able Ulster men and women who had dropped out of the negative politics of the last decade; and the overwhelming case for new thinking: "Push everything that unites in Ulster; shun everything that divides".

JAO October 1994

On Painting on Vellum

Oliver on purple sprouting broccoli. Consult Oliver before you go too far into your genealogy. Oliver is still the best man on the use of the subjunctive in modern German.

All wrong. All quite invalid. All just part of a sort of Walter Mitty land that I inhabit.

It started when we were at the Imperial Defence College in 1954. A high-up colleague confessed to me privately one day in the Ante-Room that he had this secret longing to be the recognized authority on some small area of human knowledge. Any area would do, so long as anyone else venturing on to it would feel obliged to consult him and to read his standard work and to pay tribute to him when the fellow came to write the Introduction to his patently derivative effort.

I thought the idea daft. Either you are or you are not a recognized authority; few of us can be; it is pointless to keep nursing any such ambition. Far better to get on with it.

It is a fact, for example, that we have had some delicious helpings of purple sprouting broccoli from the garden. But I wouldn't dare for a moment to hold myself out as an expert in growing that splendid vegetable. Most gardeners that I know do it much better. My plants, when you look at them, are a downright disgrace, tall, straggling, leaning over dangerously, always bursting out into pathetic little bits of yellow blossom instead of forming firm, tight heads. When showing friends round my garden, my far too big garden, that is one of my troubles. I take good care to steer their attention away from the broccoli patch, I can tell you.

As for genealogy I admit that I must have spent thousands and thousands of hours on the history of my family and of their friends and neighbours, first in my beloved County Londonderry and then away further back through the centuries in Southern Scotland, as far back indeed as 1250 when John Oliver was Prepositus of Berwick. But I have precious little to show for all that work. I remain an amateur. In the company of real genealogists or even after reading one issue of FAMILIA I keep very, very quiet. And yet it could have been such a promising field in which to display some authority.

The subjunctive in modern German? I suppose I must have had a rush of blood to the head when I was invited by the Deutsche Bau und Boden Bank in 1960 to address a big conference of German Architects, Planners, Lawyers and Financiers on the subject of the Rent Restriction Acts, about the most complex code of law in the British Statute Book at that time; and to do so in German language. The event was taking place in Bad Homburg, one of those elegant German spas with delicious food and the best of vintage Hock and Mosel. The West German top brass in those years were so polite and accommodating that they let me off lightly at Question Time and sent me home purring with contentment. Two years later they asked me to speak to them about the administration and financing of New Towns – one of our few achievements that they genuinely admired and envied. When in 1964 these nice people asked me a third time – to lecture on Slum Clearance and Redevelopment in Britain – I must have felt so flattered that the whole affair went to my head and I became quite cocky, launching out into desperately complicated sentences with finite verbs some metres distant from their syntactical masters. The audience must by then have sized me up as a charlatan for they gave me a hard time after my lecture and pestered me for an hour or more with intricate, probing questions that left me floundering, wildly spraying subjunctives, indicatives, imperatives all round the elegant salon. I was no authority. And yet the wretched seed had been sown in my mind. Some other field, perhaps, closer to home?

After I had finished my work on a philosophical analysis of the pre-suppositions and implications of the Welfare State I managed to get two or three articles published in the philosophical journals. Surely at last a recognized authority now? What better field? Why not give up my dreary old salaried job and launch out as a philosopher? A few failed applications and rejected offers sobered me up. I shrank back to my proper size.

I once got the crazy idea that I would take up Yiddish and become the greatest authority on that language between Berlin and New York, so to speak. I had been reading a lot of Jewish short stories and had been impressed by the racy, colourful use of Yiddish words and phrases – an amalgam of German, Polish and Hebrew, it seemed to me – which added enormously to the richness and the fun of those delightful stories. So, back to the Kendal and Lancaster libraries, borrowing bundles of text books and plunging in to build up a stunning vocabulary: "This Shlemiel, this Shturk, eating at a Kreplakh and a Cholla at the same time, had the chutzpa to say to me Sholem aleicha Bara ha Shem Genug shoyn." What would you have answered? But I had nobody to talk to. Nobody took the slightest interest or even listened to me, so that my new enthusiasm waned long before I could be recognized as the greatest authority on Yiddish anywhere between – where was it to be? – between Ackenthwaite and Whassett, I think I had hoped.

The Civil Service Chess Club took me by surprise when they suddenly elected me their President or Vice-President or something. An even bigger surprise burst on me when they named me First Board in their match against the Dublin Civil Service Chess Club. International Honours! Catapulted on to the world scene! Being beaten by a Fool's Mate in my first game put paid to any fancy notions I might have had of leading a great revival of chess in Ulster and becoming the recognized authority . . .

Light verse looked like a more promising field. One of my early attempts at civil service doggerel ran:

With civil servants in distress
At bad disclosures in the Press
When Ministers begin to grouse
At awkward Questions in the House
We look for stuff of fitting size
For pulling over people's eyes

And then recall the golden rule
"There is no substitute for wool".

Instead of selling that stanza at a good profit I weakly made a present of it to a fellow I knew in the wool trade – and never even got any thanks. The nearest I ever came to plagiarism, or downright theft, happened when I casually, modestly and with downcast eyes allowed people to think that the following immortal lines were mine when in fact they had been composed by a temporary war-time colleague, Professor Alan McKinnon. But then, as I say, intimations of glory go to my head. The two fellows in charge of the planned evacuation of Belfast children to the Ulster countryside in 1940 – yes, we actually judged this a necessary step even though many people were being evacuated at the same time from England to Ireland as a safe haven! – were William Duff and Jack Donaldson:

"The Duff-man and the Donaldson
Scanned the evacuees
They wept like anything to see
Such quantities of fleas.
Such nitty little Protestants
Such lousy young R.Cs."

A perfect stanza, I admitted modestly, telling a story in six lines, opening up one of the big social problems of war-time and finishing neatly with a penetrating analysis of the Ulster dichotomy.

Of course no man in his senses would ever aim to become a recognized authority on light verse. But I did find it useful to be able to string together a few rhyming couplets. You will laugh when you hear how and where that turned out to be useful – and diplomatic. Local Authorities, Local Chambers of Trade, Associations of Sanitary Officers (a splendid body of men, believe me, one of the most down-to-earth and conscientious corps of public officials) are all extremely hospitable in Ulster; and certainly in the old days of the Stormont Parliament they would generously invite a bunch of us to their Annual Dinners in various Town Halls, some ornate old Victorian edifices, some spanking modern community centres. And in fine disregard of protocol they would expect officials to make speeches as well as the Minister. Not wishing to clash or overlap with the Minister or offer any ground for comparison I used to take refuge in light verse, in sheer doggerel. Once when suddenly called on to speak in Ballymoney I actually found myself forced to work out my rhyming lines while on my feet in an effort at avoiding any clash with Terence O'Neill then our Prime Minister and Principal Speaker of the evening. I confess I knew the charming and adroit organizer, Bob Price, extremely well and was not altogether taken by surprise.

As an obscure Ulsterman I was honoured at being invited to help to supervise the Independence Elections in Rhodesia in 1980 – when Rhodesia was moving on to become Zimbabwe. I naturally swotted up all I could lay hands on concerning the detailed conduct of elections, the practical arrangements, the machinery for counting the votes and so on. This was big stuff. These elections were for real, as we said. Again I could hear the siren voice of Walter Mitty in my ear: "This is your chance to shine. You can become an Authority on Elections in the Third World and then go on to be a highly paid international consultant afterwards". In fact I soon found that the hard-working District Commissioner, Ian Rich, already knew roughly fifty times more about elections than I did and that my role was going to be a much humbler one: walking around the native townships, showing my badge, common sense, impartiality, diplomacy, holding things together, flirting with those elegant black girls and so on.

It was in Rhodesia that I brought off a social coup in the business of composing light verse, but a coup that pretty well finished me as any kind of authority. At the farewell dinner it was arranged that I should speak for the Britishers and pay a tribute to the local officials. I was glad to do so because although our relations with white Rhodesians might have been thorny and difficult, they were all right in the end. I chose to show off by speaking throughout in verse, not quite doggerel but something half-a-step higher. I remember going to some trouble to get good rhymes. For 'Kalashnikov', for example. Pride prevented me from falling back on 'thereof' or 'whereof' or any strained inversion; so I invented a new type of Election Supervisor, steeped in all the noblest traditions and liberal practices of democracy: Secretary-General Chief Commissar Georgi Oblomov. My turn to speak came late at night, after a long and more than ample dinner. I thought my bit went down well. They all laughed. Years later in a warm glow of happy, proud reminiscence, I decided to re-print my poem in something I was publishing. I had never kept copies but my friend and Rhodesian colleague John Williams of Marazion turned up the original in his garden shed there.

I was horrified. Something that I thought had sounded so well and been so happily received at midnight in 1980 seemed flat, pedestrian, plodding and utterly banal in the daylight of 1990. Not worth printing. Not worth keeping. Tear it up.

I am no authority on anything and have no ambition to be.

Having listed so many of my failures I can finally go on now to stun my readers by confessing (with one of Hilaire Belloc's more outrageous characters) that when all is said and done my weakest point is painting on vellum.

On Magilligan

It is not enough just to say that Magilligan is special. In what way is it special? What makes it special?

Geologically a raised beach Magilligan forms a most unusual triangle of land on the north coast of County Londonderry. It is entirely flat. The northern side of the triangle faces out to the Atlantic Ocean and is bounded by a curving strand some seven miles long, a beach of firm sand pounded by the huge breakers coming thundering in from America, the next parish. The western side is totally different, formed by the shore-line of Lough Foyle, a low, quiet foreshore of five miles or so where the tide goes out for half a mile and where, even then, the less salty water remains shallow for another half mile or so. The third side of the triangle, to the east and south, is formed by the northern escarpment of the big basalt plateau that stretches from the Cave Hill at Belfast, to Fair Head in County Antrim, to Benbradagh at Dungiven and then across to the cliffs overlooking Magilligan. And these cliffs in turn culminate in the striking table-top of Benevenagh, a bold, distinctive, right-angled peak dominating the whole of North Derry.

The basic soil of Magilligan, a new red sandstone, is what underlies the unique character of the area, fine, dry sand that sustains high quality grass, flowers and herbs as well as farm crops.

But no trees, no hedges, no shrubs, save for a few sally bushes that have been deliberately planted here and there.

Magilligan has always been isolated. Although lying half-way between two busy market-towns, Coleraine and Limavady, ten miles either way, it was always hard to reach till about the middle of the nineteenth century when the railway came; and later the bus. Twenty-five miles to Londonderry City – which you can just see at the head of Lough Foyle – and seventy-five miles to Belfast. And across the Lough are County Donegal and the Irish Republic.

But the stark details of that severe little geography lesson convey nothing of the real spirit of Magilligan.

The air is clear. And the song of the skylark away high up in the clear, sweet air is unforgettable. So too is the poignant cry of the peewit – the local variant of the lapwing or plover – the lonely liquid call that you never get close to but which haunts you when you go away and which catches you by the throat the moment you come back. And closer to the rocky cliffs at the Downhill end is the little tern wheeling endlessly and putting out its surprisingly sharp cry. And, all the time, depending on the weather at the moment or the weather that is on the way, the crashing sound of the big, long breakers on the golden Back Strand.

No grass anywhere that I know has the delicate scent of the Magilligan grass, laced as it is with herbs. Long before tourism became popular in Ireland, people used to come from far and near to lodge with local farmers specially for the cure – as advertised – for the benefit they received from living close to those magical qualities of medicinal herbs in good sweet grassland. The taste, the unmistakable tang, of salty ocean air added to the delicious quality of the scents and smells of this unique area.

To handle the soil, to let the soft, fine yellow sand run through your fingers, is an odd experience in the midst of farming land. Crops grow in millen sand, as they say locally, sand that is so soft and fluid that no one would imagine it could even hold up, let alone nourish, saleable crops of potatoes and oats and hay and swedes. Up till forty years ago or so a full rotation of crops was carried through – roots, cereals, beans, peas, hay and even for a time that most laborious and troublesome of crops: flax, with an even finer distinction being drawn between the slightly lower and darker parts of any one field, where potatoes would go and the higher, lighter parts of that field (not that there was much difference in reality, I always argued) where turnips would be sown. Or oats (corn as it is simply called) in the lower parts and rye (for the whiskey trade) in the higher sections. For a time after World War II carrots were thought to be worth trying in this sandy soil but the dreaded carrot-fly did too much damage. To-day it would be fairer to describe the farming more as "ranching" with cattle and sheep taking the benefit of the splendid grass.

Where farm cultivation peters out close to the sea-shore and gives way to sand-dunes this extraordinary soil still produces its own crop of dainty little dog-roses and sharp-sweet, wild strawberries in the rabbit warren. And on the sea-shore itself another crop of sea-weed, cockles, mussels and razor-shell-fish. And miles and miles of marram grass.

To the eye Magilligan has a special appeal springing from the vivid contrast between the flat, treeless plain, the black basalt cliffs and the soft rounded hills of Inishowen in County Donegal. And, all over, the sky, the great big open sky, reflecting the changing moods of the two seas beneath.

Drainage is surprisingly good for such a flat plain. For one thing the light sandy soil takes up the ample rainfall. But as well as that a series of small parallel streams – known locally as Drains, Margymonaghan Drain, Ballymagoland Drain and so on – run down from the escarpment to the sea. Much depends on the good behaviour of the central stream, the Big Drain, which in the old days used to clog and back up. I remember being taken as a child of ten or so by my grandfather Henry Sherrard of Ballymulholland to the Court House in Coleraine where, I suppose now, a Public Inquiry must have been going on into the improvement of the Big Drain and the better drainage needed all around. It seems to have worked.

Although never part of the carefully controlled Plantation of Londonderry by the London Companies under King James I – it remained "Bishop's Land" in the language of the time – Magilligan nevertheless reflects in its people the general make-up of the population of the County. The Ulster-Scots have always been the strongest element: McCracken, Morrison, Linton, Conn, Allison, Shearer or Sherrard, and so on. McLaughlin, McDermott, Quigley, McDaid, Deeny, McCorriston represented the Irish stock. At Bellarena the Heygates and at Downhill the Hervey Bruces, the two titled land-owners, took the lead with their immediate households and servants in the tiny Anglican community on the English model, even to those pathetic tablets on the walls of the nave, recalling young subalterns killed in far-away wars, pointless and irrelevant wars they seem now, looking down across empty pews in a beautiful but forlorn parish church.

But times have changed. The familiar pattern of farmer and farm labourer has been broken and Magilligan now has its full quota of doctors, lawyers, nurses, teachers and traders sensibly choosing to live in its healthy atmosphere and settled community. In a sense it is now commuter-land, providing enviable living conditions for academics at the University of Ulster in Coleraine or professional staff at the many other public boards, hospitals, schools and so on all over the northern parts of the County.

It is a peaceful area. Crime is negligible. It is hard to recall a serious disturbance apart from the occasional smuggling episode to or from the Irish Republic when prices or taxes made that a worthwhile pastime. Everyone is aware of everyone else's loyalties, of what foot he digs with, of where he went to school; but it makes little difference in practice to the daily life. The outward signs are of considerable affluence. People, left alone, go on working, travelling, buying their petrol, selling their goods and services. There is little sport, little shooting or hunting, little evident recreation. People, I suppose, have their own satisfactions. Family connections are powerful. The respect for education is immense. People go to unbelievable lengths to get their children to the big schools in Coleraine, Limavady or Londonderry and from there on to higher colleges far and wide. They know they are lucky to have such choices open to them.

One of the signs, I always think, of a truly settled community is the way in which it can absorb an intrusion however threatening it may seem. When the British War Office, for example, set up a Camp in Magilligan for summer training and manoeuvres some of us thought that the quiet peaceful Magilligan that we loved would be ruined for ever. Not at all. By leaving the Army to their own devices on the one hand and on the other trading quietly with the commissariat in butter, milk and eggs the local people came out well. The arrival more recently of a Prison threatened to destroy the peace in an even more unhappy way; but once more a necessary intrusion was quietly absorbed.

I have always been intrigued by the lively connection between such a remote, rural and (one might imagine) backward area and the big world of education and employment. Again and again that connection strikes those of us who are in love with the place. You do not need to live for ever in the neighbourhood. You may go away and live far off; you may have a career in aeronautics or accountancy or commerce that takes you far away into the wider world. But you belong to the place nevertheless. You are part of it, still. It is a matter of people as well as place, of spirit as well as soil.

Magilligan is a modest place. It does not waste time telling you about famous people who came from the parish. One was a blind harpist who played before Princes. One was Lord Moran who became Mr. Churchill's Physician. But I enjoy myself tracing other odd connections that I think I can conjure up. When we were small children playing in Ballymulholland we used to set up imaginary houses among the sandhills and prepare imaginary meals. Dinner consisted of raw potato sliced into cold water and of course attracted no takers – except one, John McDaid, a great big labouring man, one of the humblest of a humble tribe. To his eternal credit John McDaid flattered us by eating our "dinners", actually chewing and swallowing the raw potato sliced into cold water. Judge our pleasure and pride to-day, seventy or eighty years on, when BBC Radio Four produces Father John McDaid, leading Jesuit thinker and writer, to give us "Thought For The Day" that – I think I can discern – includes a perceptive word on rural Ulster.

The hold that Magilligan has on me comes not only from the five senses that I have touched on here but from deeper sources as well, sources that are human and spiritual and perhaps even more powerful.

One of the greatest benefits to our whole family living in industrial and commercial Belfast was the direct, ready and highly personal contact we had with the farming life in Magilligan. My Mother's parents wanting to support their daughter in the big city kept an open door for her and her seven children. So also did her brothers Tom and Harry. But supreme among them all was Tom's Inishowen wife, our Aunt Isobel, the very embodiment of generosity, hospitality and totally care-free welcome – one of the most remarkable and memorable women in the huge gallery of our family connection. "You City folk" she would cry as she saw us modestly picking at one small potato on the dinner-table and up-ended the big dish of laughing, splitting, floury Up-to-Dates or Arran Banners on to the table for us to enjoy. She made us work, as well, an experience that taught us a lot about animals, crops, procreation, the sequence of the seasons. The crowded happy, memories of those fruitful days bind us to Magilligan in a way that little else could do.

But there are deeper roots. This North Derry coast is the homeland of Olivers, Sherrards, Morrells and all the other branches of our enormous tribe. I see the traces at every turn, running back to the year 1600 at least.

There are still deeper attachments. While the attractions of the five senses are very real, there is for me an even greater attraction in something else, something that has lasted longer than the farms, the family or even the community. The hold that the land and the people have on me is never so strong as the hold of the open air, the sea-shore, the tide, the lonely estuary. It is here that nature moves my soul more powerfully than anything else. The effect is no longer just physical or psychological or intellectual; it is spiritual. The vast expanse. The solitude. The empty strand. The everlasting mystery of the tide at ebb and flow. The big rain clouds blowing up from the western hills. The ineffable blue of the sky once the rain has washed it clean again. The haunting cry of the sea-birds. Love is heaven and heaven love.

Some small-minded reader will say that I exaggerate. Some unfortunate reader who has never written a full-blooded love-letter or – worse still – has never received one, will allege that in this frank and uninhibited love-letter to Magilligan it is a sad case of John once again going Over The Top, complete with his well-known rose-tinted spectacles.

But there is more to be said.

The other day I turned up a 1966 Survey of Magilligan sent to me by my old friend Joe Frey, whom I had helped to welcome as a refugee from Central Europe to Ulster in the 1930s. Writing from The Queen's University of Belfast where he was head of Extra-Mural Studies he had added a foreword to a symposium of extremely learned articles by the Route Naturalists Field Club.

Where I happen to mention in passing the growth of some herbs in the Magilligan grass, the Survey speaks of Magilligan as "the medicine garden of Europe". Where I mention the skylark and the peewit, the Survey lists some ninety species of birds with details of their varied habitats "which makes the area unique in Ulster". I forgot to mention butterflies, simply taking for granted the happy sightings of a Painted Lady or a Small Tortoiseshell in the stack-garden; the Survey lists sixteen, by Latin and by popular names. Twenty varieties of moth are recorded in "this most important area". Where I mention, I think, three sea-shells, the Survey finds no fewer than eighty types of gastropod on the Back Strand alone, between Downhill and The Point. Where I recall a couple of wild flowers, the Survey records something like four hundred flowering plants, including Salix Repens (the finest specimen seen anywhere) and a climbing madder plant carrying the Sherrard name.

When I was a small boy, my grandfather and my uncles in Ballymulholland used to impress on me the great importance of putting on both my boots before beginning to lace up either one of them. To lace up one boot before putting on the other was sure to bring misfortune. According now to the Route Naturalists it was no less a person than St.Columb himself – my favourite saint – who laid down that golden rule in the Magilligan or Tamlaghtard where he spent much time founding the monastery at Duncrun and preparing to go to the historic Convention of Drumceatt nearby in the year 575 A.D.

One day, some thirty years ago now, a well-known farmer died, tragically killed by a passing motor-bicycle. He had been jolly, gay, musical, the most musical of his tribe by far. As the huge crowd of mourners stood around his small farmhouse away down near to the lonely Magilligan Point, the voice of the Presbyterian Minister rose in the clear sweet air, saying:

"They told me, Heraclitus, they told me you were dead,
They brought me bitter news to hear and bitter tears to shed,
I wept as I remembered how often you and I
Had tired the sun with talking and sent him down the sky.
Still are thy pleasant voices, thy nightingales awake,
For death he taketh all away but them he cannot take".

Even death will not separate us from Magilligan.

On a Big City with Big Ideas

In a thoughtful article recently in the Town Planning Journal Dr.William Neill of The Queen's University of Belfast analysed the power of town planning to influence the current drive for "re-imaging" the City of Belfast as well as the limits to that power. He was penetrating on the popular aim of getting back a semblance of normality after twenty years of ceaseless IRA bombing. "Normality" may be one of the worthy aims of English Ministers under Direct Rule; but what in fact is "normality" in a city of sharply divided loyalties? Is it merely "lipstick on the face of the gorilla"? I was glad to see Dr.Neill stressing the real divisions which, as I have always maintained, are ethnic, cultural and political. To drive home that point Dr.Neill included a most telling photograph of a street in East Belfast dominated by the Goliath Cranes of the shipyard (note the name!) and carrying on a wall the merciless slogan:-

"IRISH OUT
THE ULSTER CONFLICT IS ABOUT NATIONALITY"

"Other newspapers please copy", as the Belfast Telegraph used to say for the benefit of Ulster men and women in North America. I would add "Radio and Television as well, please, whether or not the slogan and its message fit your pre-conceived image of Belfast".

But in the course of his analysis the writer quoted the Ulster poet John Hewitt as suggesting that what was needed in Belfast was "to construct a new mythology of the city". A pretty strange phrase, I thought; but then I never believed that John Hewitt's worldliness came anywhere near to the quality of his verse, his happy rhythms and his moving rural images.

Trying to construct a new mythology may indeed be a nonsense, a contradiction, an oxymoron of a foolish kind; but, more charitably, let us say that we know what our poet meant.

Let us pick out some facts in the history and culture of this vivid, challenging City and let us see whether they reveal something of its spirit and help us to get away from the older myths. It may turn out to be more a matter of re-imagining the city than re-imaging.

When we were little boys running around the streets of Ballynafeigh or swinging from those elegant Edwardian street lamp-posts, we used to boast about our city: we had the biggest shipyard in the world, we said, the biggest linen factory in the world, the biggest rope works, the biggest gas works, the biggest tobacco factory. Everything had to be the biggest. Nothing less would do.

As time went on I came to see that that was not just the phantasy of little boys but was characteristic of many phases in our history and many aspects of the life we actually led in this city of paradoxes.

My quietly perceptive colleague Gilbert Camblin struck this very note at the beginning of his much under-rated book "The Town in Ulster". The official arrangements for the Plantation of Ulster made under King James the First in 1609 were both detailed and ambitious. They added up to a strategic Regional Plan, no less, and were far from being merely a panic measure to meet some short-term political need. Camblin, a Town Planner, found in the Plantation the biggest example of regional planning anywhere in or near its time. Perhaps if it had been even bigger and if, in Planning language, development control had matched plan-making, it might have succeeded in producing a happier settlement for all concerned. But big it certainly was for 1609.

(My wife and I have been amused that all of our sons turned out to be geographers at heart whatever other skills they may have acquired; like us they constantly seek to match the physical landscape with the human endeavour so as to build up for themselves some picture of life and work wherever in the world they happen to find themselves. Apart from its intrinsic fascination, geography is a synthesis rather than an analysis and, as such, a lot more constructive. In that sense geography can make a more positive contribution to understanding society than can endless analysis. And as a life-long enthusiast for town and country planning I insist that geography represents the true basis for town and country planning to a much greater and healthier extent than does architecture or engineering or sociology or economics.)

In no time seventeenth-century Belfast, the big developing sea-port elbowed the port of Carrickfergus out of its way and brought sea-going ships right into the middle of the town. The river Lagan soon needed bridging and in the late 1600s one of the biggest structures of its kind in the British Isles was erected: The Long Bridge, 2,562 feet long with twenty-one arches. As the putative builder of the nine-arch Devorguilla Bridge over the river Nith in Dumfries, in the thirteenth century Magister John Oliver may be allowed a special interest in such grandiose structures.

Sir Charles Brett's fascinating book: "Buildings of Belfast" harps on this same theme again and again. No sycophant, no yes-man, no apologist Brett critically examines churches, factories, warehouses, public buildings, private houses, schools, pubs and so on with the benefit of personal research, sharp observation and acid comment. He presents the buildings of Belfast repeatedly as robust, vigorous, splendiferous, rugged and determined, wholly astonishing.

And such big affairs are still in vogue to-day. I know of no other city so ringed around with splendiferous new bungalows adorned with massive ranch-style fencing.

Sixty-six thousand tons displacement, eleven stories high, a sixth of a mile long: by any measurement the Titanic was an enormous ship, the biggest of her time when she was built in Belfast in 1911. Her tragic end might have been expected to put a stop to the building of big ships in the Queen's Island; but not a bit. The Canberra and countless big container vessels followed in due course.

The founders of Belfast Inst, the liberal merchants of the city after the Act of Union, had big ideas when they set out in the early 1800s to create a completely new institution in the heart of their city. Their aims were once again ambitious: "a complete, uniform and extensive system of education" with "access to the higher branches of learning as well as those which would fit youths for a commercial career."

What they set up in 1810 was not only a fiercely independent and non-sectarian grammar school but also a university college at one and the same time and under the same roof. Not exactly a modest undertaking. Something of the same bigness of spirit has persisted at Inst ever since. Sticking it out as a "B" School under the Schools Settlement of 1947 Inst even to-day eschews Government Grant on its capital works and manages, by its own efforts, to add an enormous common hall and a spacious sixth form centre to Sir John Soane's elaborate 1810 designs.

And you can see the essence of the same big idea all around. The Housing Executive could well claim to be the biggest house-building public agency in the Kingdom if it were so minded. And the Eastern Board is held up as the biggest health authority in many respects. Nothing, but nothing, can surpass the extensive and efficient network of modern roads and bridges, one of the best examples anywhere of the happy marriage of big political aims with rolls-royce administration. For my part I regret none of all this. The best way to progress administratively – I stress administratively – in Ulster has been proven time and time again to lie away from local parochial animosities and in the direction of big well-staffed bodies. And, goodness knows, the whole Province is a small enough place in itself. There is ample room for smallness in other spheres in Ulster.

Every hill is a mountain, every village a town. The Belfast Festival at Queen's is billed every November as the biggest arts festival in Britain after Edinburgh.

Maybe this obsession with bigness reflects some sort of burning inferiority in our hearts and results in a compelling need to puff out our chests? I hardly think so, as there are many instances that are harder to explain.

In 1961, in answer to a particularly dreary phase in the long saga of extending the Belfast City Boundary – most people thought that the city was big enough already in relation to the small province while the City Fathers thought otherwise – Sir Robert Matthew (a leading Edinburgh architect and town-planner) was called in to advise. It fell to me to make the arrangements. And the outcome, far from simply fiddling with the details of the city boundary here and there, was a stunning surprise: a big regional plan, curbing the growth of the city, setting a stop-line to further city growth, building up a necklace of growth towns (Bangor, Lisburn, Antrim etc) and giving us not just a new town (which were two-a-penny in those days) but a new regional city. – in all, a regional plan that was certainly big in its vision and conception.

But of course people said (and alas in Ireland there are always people standing ready to pull down their dearest friends) that those were not the ideas of Robert Matthew the visiting expert; they alleged that I had unduly influenced him and egged him on to put these grandiose ideas into his Plan. That would have been a serious over-estimate of my abilities and a gross offence to the integrity of Robert Matthew. But, as often happens, that pathetic little controversy did disclose a small grain of truth of another kind. Matthew came to Belfast not knowing much about the place and no doubt harbouring some pretty poor impressions from the outside. After two or three years of intensive work on the ground he changed some of his views. He got to know the place and to like it. He was captivated by the people and by the atmosphere. He became one of us and came back again and again. His name passed into the language. People spoke of the Matthew Stop-Line and the Matthew towns, even of some development having been "Matthewed". Ireland once again had absorbed the invader, who then went on to give us the big treatment.

I think I can trace something of the same change in the experience of many great men who came to work in Belfast. I think for instance of some with whom I happen to have worked: Lord Scarman, General Kitson, Maurice Oldfield of MI5 or was it MI6, Sir Edmund Compton the Ombudsman, Sir James Dunnett the Permanent Secretary of Defence, all of whom at least came to understand the city and its problems much better after working there. Is it any wonder that I have constantly asked for a lot more secondment, interchange and mobility of that kind? And there are amongst my closest colleagues many outstanding examples of able and distinguished English and Scottish men and women who made Ulster not only their home but the object of their affections and of their great abilities.

A fine example of that kind of mature Ulster experience is represented by Professor Sir Charles Carter who from his altruistic life and sheer hard work in Ulster developed a frankly critical understanding combined with a genuine sympathy for the Ulster people, all of them. And yet here was someone with a thoroughly English upbringing and education and of course the highest British academic and administrative standards. Is it any wonder that I constantly ask for a lot more imports and exchanges of that sort, in both directions, a lot more fluidity in employment and in influence, to help counterbalance the endless litany of complaint, grievance and accusation?

Anent the big idea being planted in Ulster by someone who is not by any reckoning an Ulsterman, or who has not grown up in the peculiar psychology of Ulster or who has no need whatever to share any feeling of inferiority, I keep my best example to the end. Here is someone from outside the Province, a Scot, a scientist, an administrator who comes to Belfast as a stranger, takes on a hard job in the heart of the city and makes a success of it. In his yearly letter to graduates the Vice-Chancellor of The Queen's University of Belfast regularly does two things which I greatly admire. He seeks to keep graduates all over the world in touch with their University and with its remarkable achievements, fulfilling one of the great needs of Ulster – extending the concept of Ulster and of being "Ulster" far and wide, as I constantly advocate. But he also blows our trumpet for us in a way that is soundly based, novel and worthwhile. In his 1992 letter Dr.Gordon Beveridge tells us all about the revolutionary abolition of "Finals" at Queen's, about the two Semesters that replace the old three Terms and about the modularizing of University teaching. More than that, Queen's is amongst the few Universities in Britain to succeed in making such big changes. He argues the great advantages that are likely to flow. And he puffs out our chests as well. He reminds us that Queen's admitted her first woman student as long ago as 1881 and her first woman medical student away back in 1889. "Now, as then" he goes on "The mainland is looking to us for guidance as they follow, at a slower pace, along a similar path."

That's the stuff. I'm all for the big idea and the big approach. The biggest shipyard in the world . . .

On Playing Rugby Football

The wet soggy ball squirted back from some loose play just inside the enemy Twenty-Five and close to the touch-line where I happened to be watching. By chance it came to one of our heroes – Billy Hall – who in a split second spun round and kicked a drop-goal, thus earning a valuable four points for Instonians in their struggle against North.

I was astonished and deeply impressed. Up till that moment – it must have been 1925 or so, when I was twelve – I had innocently believed that a drop-goal could be scored only from a position in front of the posts and that somehow the Laws of the game permitted nothing else. But much more importantly the episode of kicking a goal with a wet, heavy ball from an acute angle impressed on me for life the value of skilful kicking in Rugby.

Pretentious but superficial commentators make a great error in over-stressing the fact that Rugby is "a handling code" and deploring the use of "the boot". Of course good crisp handling and passing can be a delight to watch and are part of the glory of the game. And good handling can include a range of elegant variations – the straight pass, the reverse pass, the dummy, the scoop, the flip, the long pass, the smuggled pass, the scissors and so on. but even when one includes putting-in to the scrum and throwing-in to the line-out one can scarcely reckon more than a dozen handling movements. Twenty-five, by contrast, is my tally for kicking, when every variation is remembered such as the garryowen, the grubber, the little chip and – my much lamented favourite – the dribble.

Why has the dribble dropped out of fashion? At school we were actually taught how to dribble. Once, for instance, the Irish International Billy Ross spent a strenuous hour or so at Osborne Park, drilling some of us from Pirrie House in the arts of grouping closely together and dribbling in a controlled way. Again and again now-a-days I see a six-foot-three forward bending down to pick up a spinning ball in the loose only to fumble it, knock on and cause the game to be stopped. Far better surely to take the ball on with his feet when, especially if supported by one or two of his friends, he would be well-nigh unstoppable. Do not tell me that it cannot be done. I have seen it at least once in modern times, at Ravenhill, when Mike Gibson in his great days dribbled along the touch-line in front of the Stand and gained fully forty or fifty metres on his own. If he could do it and if the Laws permitted, then why cannot others? My conclusion simply is that Mike Gibson had all the skills.

Well-meaning commentators still deplore the scoring of points and (as they unconvincingly allege) the winning of matches by the despicable method of kicking penalty goals. Some, like Andy Irvine of Scotland, himself a champion goal-kicker, have gone so far as to say that they would like to see the goal-posts abolished and all point-scoring by kicking done away with. This fails to deal properly with the obvious need to punish offences and fails to do justice to the art and practice of skilful kicking in what is, after all, Rugby Football.

Players, coaches and administrators of to-day will obviously have their own ideas on all those matters, based on much better knowledge than I have. That is beyond question. But it may do no harm if, for once, an onlooker from the unreserved embankment offers some comparisons between the game of to-day and the game of seventy years ago. Allow me, for example, to smile when I hear a commentator, watching a scrum-half, on a windy day, lying down and steadying a place-kick with one finger, liken the action to the practice of scrum-halves "in the old days". Little do they know. In the real old days, as I know from hard experience, the scrum-half had to hold the ball off the ground with both his hands and place it down on the earth only when the kicker's boot came within an inch or two. We were tough, then.

Rugby is played widely and enthusiastically in Ulster, mainly in the Grammar Schools but in some Comprehensives as well, with Masters still giving much of their spare time to supporting the Physical Education Instructors. Then the players move on to the Senior Clubs, which are at the heart and soul of the game. Although Ravenhill, the official Headquarters, is a bare, cheerless ground, it still remains the great venue for all major occasions in Ulster Rugby. It may be cheerless – there is precious little comfort even in the Stand – but it has the great compensating virtues of being safe, spacious and (with the enviable road system) easily reached within minutes from any part of the Belfast area. When in the early 1970s, I think it was, Ewart Bell, Dudley Higgins and other elder statesmen in the Ulster Branch considered spending some of their limited funds on cheering up Ravenhill they came down against any such plan, confirming the widely-held conviction that the Clubs remained the kernel of the game and that any money that might be available would be better spent there. In quite a different context creeping commercialism may now be forcing changes to be made in the shape of "corporate hospitality facilities" at Ravenhill. I think I spotted something of that kind last time I was there, watching the All Blacks thrash Ulster.

To real followers of the game it matters little whether Ravenhill, once you get there, is prettified with lawns and flower-beds. It is the match, the contest, the confrontation on the pitch that matters. Just pay a visit on St.Patrick's Day when the World and His Wife are cheering on their school in that great sporting event, the Ulster Schools Cup final. Here is Rugby at its keenest and brightest, with fit, healthy, intelligent young men, well-taught, totally amateur, playing their hearts out with total commitment and (as many have told me privately, for I never came near to reaching any representative side) with enormous pride in representing the School they love in front of class-mates, teachers, governors, parents, old boys and all shapes and sizes and genders of supporters. Once, when attending with my family the Military Tattoo in Edinburgh Castle on the last night of the Festival, I found myself in a dramatic setting with spectators stacked up in darkness on all sides of the Esplanade and with an empty, swept arena brightly flood-lit as we waited expectantly for some military display. I then heard Simon, in the Fourth Form, whisper to me "I'd give anything to see the Inst First Fifteen run out there just now." I agreed with him.

One of the many ways in which Rugby in Ulster has changed over the years is the way in which strength has spread outside Belfast to the provincial towns. It used to be that the real rivalry was between Methody, Academy, Campbell and Inst, the four big Belfast grammar schools with only an occasional invasion by Portora from Enniskillen or by Coleraine Inst. Now fully twenty schools offer serious challenge and add spice to the competition. In the same way, and to some extent as a result, Senior Clubs from all over the Province are in the front rank and enrich the game.

It may be thought far-fetched and fanciful to link those changes in the geography of the game with the Matthew Plan for Physical Development of Ulster in the early 1960s; but the two are linked. For those of us who watched that Plan – curbing the growth of Belfast, boldly drawing a total Stop-line around it, deliberately building up Growth Towns at Bangor, Newtownards, Lurgan, Portadown, Ballymena and so on – there is a quiet satisfaction in seeing the human and social consequences of that courageous Plan now manifest in the vitality and prominence of Rugby Clubs at Bangor, Ards, Ballymena, Dungannon and so on.

Whereas we used to get some International Rugby at Ravenhill we no longer do, because the Irish Rugby Football Union very sensibly decided some thirty or forty years ago to concentrate their funds on Landsdowne Road in Dublin, drawing bigger crowds there and making the International events more accessible from all parts of the island. It is a matter of great satisfaction that in attending at Ravenhill and Lansdowne Road well over a couple of hundred times in seventy years I have never, ever, seen any crowd disturbance or trouble. As support for the game has widened some of the old niceties have, alas, declined such as applauding good play by the visitors or keeping quiet while a place-kick at goal is being taken. New spectators boo anything they don't like. That is a pity; but the decline is trivial compared with the awful deterioration in crowd behaviour at big Cricket Matches in England where the noise is insufferable and a posse of police is needed to protect the playing strip from vandalism during intervals.

The fact that at Ravenhill in modern times we get only Inter-Provincial Rugby and Home Matches for Ulster receiving touring sides from Australia, New Zealand, South Africa and so on is a loss but not, in my view, a total loss. Ulster stands high and often comes out the champion Province of the four Irish Provinces. There is much truth in the saying "When Ulster is strong, Ireland is strong." And the absence of full Five-Nations-Championship Matches means at any rate that we are spared watching some very boring play by England (however successful) and incidentally also that we are spared those awful National Anthems. It is surely high time some sensible people in the Home Unions took that problem in hand and tactfully recommended either the abolition of the nonsensical practice or the choice all round of more fitting and less offensive songs. The last man to stir up trouble I confine myself merely to mentioning the gross insensitivity of England singing "God Save The Queen" when facing the Scots at Murrayfield; the Scots in Dublin singing "Flower of Scotland" with its misplaced and tasteless references; the Ulstermen in the Irish side seen standing dumb and tight-lipped while "The Soldier's Song" is chanted at Twickenham. A little tact and maturity all round, please.

Television manages to suggest that Rugby consists largely of heavy men heaving and pushing and piling up mindlessly. Have the producers and cameramen really tried hard enough to give us more, in long-shot, of the pattern of the game, the movement off the ball, the way in which some gifted players can anticipate the run of play and, like Trevor Ringland for example, when attacking on the right wing suddenly bring off a match-saving tackle on the left wing? This is where one of the many glories of the game could be picked up and displayed to the watching world. Although television is technically brilliant I still get greater satisfaction from a seat high up in the Stand or even standing on the crest of the unreserved banking whence I can take my own mental pictures of the ebb and flow of the whole of the game at its most intelligent.

Out of touch now with the politics and personalities of the game I cannot attempt to interpret the poor showing of Ireland in the statistics of the international game. Going simply by what I see – sparkle, dash, success in the first half followed by obvious fatigue and failure in the second half – I dare to suggest that that pattern reflects much of the ethos of the game in Ireland. You play with enthusiasm, flair, originality but don't trouble too much with the heavy coaching, the solemn planning and the fearsome physical training that other countries go in for. In some ways the pattern of rugby that I see reflects in an odd sense the pattern of amateur play production that I have spoken about elsewhere – not too fussy about sets and costumes but gifted in acting and production. The pattern recalls also the account given so many times by Bill Beaumont: "In the first twenty minutes the green jerseys come at you from so many angles that you get the impression the Irish are fielding thirty men, not fifteen".

Even though beaten so often Ireland may possibly be closer to the spirit of the game than other countries are. Add the unhappy saga of financial rewards to players and England, for example, may find the spirit and the fun beginning to evaporate. Still, I want to see my side winning more often and as an Ulsterman I confess my pulse beats faster when I see those green Irish jerseys run out on to any pitch.

Pattern, anticipation, balanced running add up to an aspect of Rugby that far transcends any image of the plodding around of a muddied oaf. A brilliant example was shown to those of us lucky enough to be at Murrayfield on March 16, 1991, when Scotland were entertaining Ireland in what turned out to be the most delightful International game in recent years. Keith Crossan receiving the ball on the left wing and expected by all of us to go hard and straight for the corner flag boldly decided to cut inside and with a dazzling display of light, clever, twinkle-toed running – he passed several defenders without ever seeming to touch the ground – danced his way through to score a try under the posts. It was Rugby at its best. It was genius. It was ballet.

Most Rugby-playing countries have their tales of rugby "running in families" but few more prominently and more lastingly than Ulster with the Hewitt family. When I went up to Inst the talk was still of Tom and Frank Hewitt, a few years ahead of me, playing for Ireland and both of them scoring in their first matches. Frank actually played for Ireland while still a schoolboy at Inst. (In case there should possibly be a reader anywhere in the English-speaking world who still does not know what is meant by "Inst" let me say factually, impartially and with commendable restraint that Inst is the familiar and affectionate term for the greatest Grammar School in the British Isles, the Royal Belfast Academical Institution. I am sorry to have to spell out such a banal, threadbare and well-established fact, but there it is). Tom and Frank were followed by Hamilton Hewitt playing both Rugby and Soccer at top level, Victor, Norman and, in the next generation, Stanley and Austin as well as David Hewitt a British Lion described by Tony O'Reilly as "the finest runner with a Rugby ball I have ever played with". Hewitts, they are now an enormous clan including Edgar and Gerry Gilpin, still keep appearing on rugby grounds all over Ireland.

Some time in the 1970s, I think it must have been, I happened to be standing at the touch-line watching Instonians play Malone in a needle end-of-season match. Just in front of me the ball came back quite unexpectedly to my friend and fellow Governor John Hewitt – exactly where Billy Hall had received it fifty or so years earlier. Playing, as I seem to remember, in his last game of senior club Rugby John Hewitt spun round and kicked a drop goal from the touch-line and well inside the enemy Twenty-two, scoring for his side the mere three points now given by a niggardly set of Laws for that most dramatic of football achievements, the unexpected drop-goal, from an un-likely distance, at an impossible angle.

On Learning from Boys Clubs and other Modest Affairs

"The 130 members, who are Protestants and Catholics in equal numbers, fully justify the policy of the club by the sincere and friendly way in which they work and play together with never the slightest trace of sectarianism or intolerance."

That is a quotation from the 22nd Annual Report of the Belfast Newsboys Club printed and published in March 1948.

The reader might be pardoned for reaching for a pinch of salt if that statement had been put out by a politician or another activist keen to push some propaganda. But it was written by St.Clair Gilroy, the Club Leader, a man of the people, a most down-to-earth social worker, extremely close to his area and his people. His catchment area was the network of small mean streets off York Street, Corporation Street and Upper Queen Street, then some of the poorest in Ulster. The poverty of those boys, Catholic and Protestant equally, was illustrated with brutal candour by an announcement printed on the back cover of the same Report: "Many of the boys are very poorly clad and left-off clothing will be gratefully accepted by the club for distribution among the members. Boots and shoes to fit boys aged 14–18 will be specially welcomed." One can picture the scene: boys selling the Belfast Telegraph each evening on the rain-soaked streets, bare-footed or more probably in shoes that let in and were long past any hope of repair. Catholic and Protestant equally. Fortunately economic conditions have improved out of all recognition since 1948; but it is the political aspect that is still relevant.

In all my visits to the Newsboys in those years during and after the War I do not seem, somehow, to recall bumping into any British or American news reporters investigating that splendid example of decent work; nor dewy-eyed young English girls tripping over one another to devote themselves to the valuable endeavour – as (since violence started in 1969) all of them have been prominent in doing at say, Corrymeela, our leading example of ecumenical co-operative effort. While Corrymeela and the many other modern schemes are to be welcomed and supported for their greater depth and more thoughtful concern I insist on pointing out, in all factual accuracy, that similar efforts at bridging the divide within the poorest and most flammable sections of society were flourishing long before Corrymeela had been heard of. Even away back in 1938 the Social Service Society of Civil Servants at Stormont had been hard at work on totally non-sectarian lines. Far from laying down any self-conscious rules or quotas or percentages the Civil Servants (in their private, off-duty capacity) simply went ahead as if the questions of religion and politics did not affect their work on the back streets of West Belfast. Or long before that again the Belfast Girls Club Union under the leadership of those remarkable ladies Frances Heron and Anastasia McCready; their response to any suggestion of religious sectarianism would have been devastating. To those of us who stick to the facts of history the awful decline in community spirit and cohesiveness since 1969 is all the more galling.

For those many conscientious people who strove hard in their different ways to build up an integrated society in Ulster it is now bitter beyond words to see much of their work undone in the present hateful political atmosphere. Those in Great Britain who understand and sympathize with the physical and economic sufferings of the Ulster people caused by the IRA and reflected by the brutal retaliation and revenge of the extreme Loyalists can have little idea how deep the mental and moral sufferings run. What's the use? Aren't we all helpless now? – thus run the sad murmurings of people who worked hard for a better future that is slow in coming and indeed seems further away than ever. Their sufferings deserve a lot more thought and sympathy than they get.

For eight years or so after the War I acted as Chairman of the Federation of Boys Clubs in Northern Ireland, with something like fifty affiliated clubs all over the Province. Some like Long Tower and St.Eugene's in Londonderry or St.John Bosco in Newry were run by the Catholic Church. Some like St.Mary's on the Crumlin Road by the Episcopal Churches League. Lombard by the Irish Temperance League. And then all the non-denominational clubs.

Everywhere around me in the social field I saw clubs, societies and associations rise and as quickly fall again with the personality and energy of one live wire: – the Secretary – Organiser or the Organising Secretary, the all-purpose chief officer expected to carry the organisation on his or her own shoulders with whatever help he or she could muster. Again and again I watched one or other of two things happen. An enthusiast would be rushing around keenly driving the fieldwork ahead, but neglecting the paper work, letting the money get into a muddle, making diplomatic or political gaffes, never staying in the office long enough to answer letters, available in practice only to some sectors, leaving others to feel ignored. Or, an officer would be conscientiously looking after the office, keeping a close eye on the money, seeing that every letter was attended to, keeping good records, but tied to the desk and failing to get out and push the real purposes of the organisation.

Both situations can be the despair of the official bodies they have to deal with. Both situations are responsible for the low esteem in which voluntary organisations are often held. Both are answerable for the seeming reluctance of Government Departments to hand out grants of taxpayer's money.

I am prepared to believe that there are voluntary bodies lucky enough to have one exceptional top person who can combine the two necessary attributes, administrative wisdom and balance on the one hand and on the other physical energy and infectious enthusiasm; but I cannot say that I have come across a great many.

It did not take long working with the boys clubs in Ulster to size up the problem and think of a solution.

Divide the job. Appoint a Secretary to run the office, service the committee and guard the money. Appoint separately an Organiser, an enthusiast, a specialist, to get out into the field, visit all areas and press ahead with the essential aims of the work. Let each have in his job specification a clear duty to think of the other and to meet his needs. And if, as I know many people fear, there is still thought to be a danger in having two bosses, then there is a role for the Chairman or Vice Chairman or some designated Committee member to make it his business to see both the Secretary and the Organiser together, at intervals, and help to set the course as part of the whole pattern of management.

We were lucky in the Federation of Boys Clubs to get as our Secretary a splendid man, Vince Dunlop, who grasped those principles sturdily and stayed with us a long time. He made it his job to steer matters so that the Organiser – a succession of keen young men who stayed only a few years before moving on to higher spheres – felt free to give all his energies to getting out, stirring up the dust of new ideas in the secure knowledge that the Secretary would always be there to settle the dust and do the tidying up.

Once when travelling on holiday in a bus through Myroe in deepest rural Londonderry I met an enthusiastic young girl, Elizabeth, who was mad keen to set up a Youth Club but who needed a lot of advice and had no idea where to find it. As I stepped off the bus in Magilligan at five o'clock I spotted a telephone kiosk. A call found Vince Dunlop at his desk, as I knew it would. Packing up a few leaflets, scribbling a quick letter and promising an early visit by the Organiser he got the envelope into the late posting box at the Head Post Office in Royal Avenue on his way home to the Cliftonville Road. It reached Elizabeth next morning on the remote farm where she lived on the Lough Foyle shore; and it met her needs. Our reputation shot up. Under any orthodox system I should have been unlikely to find the Organiser in the office; a clerk would have offered "to ring me back"; and would have been too unsure of herself to decide which leaflets to send out, feeling she had to wait for instructions from the great man who, she would have thought, had perhaps already been to that very area but did not always have time to tell her where he had been or what contacts he had made.

Those are but trivial cameos of what a good independent Secretary can do. The very fact that he is independent of the enthusiast is important in itself. It gives him the standing to size up, to comment, to criticize, to warn, to encourage. Any sensible Organiser worth his salt will see the value of that sort of arrangement to him and to the work he is keen to promote. In any case it helps any of us to be able to talk over our worries with an equal and quietly take counsel. The presence of a good Secretary-Administrator can also help to give stability and permanence to a body whereas, by their very nature, enthusiasts have a habit of coming and going.

I am certain that the separation of duties in the way I describe is the best solution in many situations in the voluntary field or the "independent" field as it is perhaps more often called now-a-days in Ulster. But I am equally certain that that advice is not often followed, people harbouring a deep conviction that it is basically wrong to have "two bosses". May I gently suggest that these people ask themselves the further question: Who is the true boss? for many arrogantly ignore the truth that the true boss is the elected committee. Clearly there is room for different approaches. Modern management theories no doubt have their answers – all I ask is that mine be given a hearing.

Carrying the argument over for a moment into the management of schools working under local management and with their own budgets, there is a big difference between those schools which have a separate and recognized Bursar (under whatever name) and those who have to look to the Head for advice and action on every problem. It can be pathetic to watch a Head feebly struggling to explain to his Governors some intricate questions about pensions (and they can be fiendish) or floundering over some breach of legal contract. Some Heads are so obsessed with the golden image of "The Great Headmaster enjoying the total confidence of his Governors" that they are actually jealous of any competition offered, or even suspected, from an able Bursar. This of course is a total misconception. A good Bursar knows that in the eyes of the pupils, staff and parents the Head is the embodiment of the school *and must be*; the wise Bursar keeps himself and his work quietly and tactfully in the background. That, after all, is one of the arts of good administration.

To get back to the Boys Clubs. They were modest affairs in my day, working in execrable premises in the back streets. I hope they are enjoying decent facilities to-day. When I was in the habit of visiting them I was always impressed by one truth, the drive imparted to the Clubs by having any one aim, any one sense of common purpose. Two were outstanding: football and boxing. I learned that all differences melted away in face of the ups and downs of their Football League or their Boxing Trophies – prestige, length of existence, politics, geography counting for little. Winning was all.

The further service the Boys Clubs did for me was to give me the feeling, the true unvarnished feeling of the least advantaged parts of society, in town and in country, raw perhaps, but vigorous, frank and above all warm. The fact that the Organiser was free to get around all the member clubs meant that he was able to take me into homes in remote areas of Ulster that I might never otherwise have got to know, even though I was an Ulsterman through and through. That is why I was happy to stay eight years in the job and why I gave it up only because I had to leave Belfast to go to the Imperial Defence College, then the leading military academy in the British Commonwealth.

Boys Clubs with their informal atmospheres and total absence of uniform or rank appeal to many boys who are put off by the rituals and behaviour of the Boy Scouts. But I am now coming to appreciate more and more clearly the continuing, long-term success of the Boys Brigade in Ulster – well over two hundred flourishing B.B.Companies to-day. This seems to confirm that for many boys there is still a great appeal in discipline, order, rank and smart appearance, as well as in the Christian message. Girls, certainly in the times I am speaking of for the most part, were looked on as much less "clubbable" than boys. But I dare say that that attitude has changed along with so much else in the social revolution which we are going through in our generation – and a real revolution it is, in Ulster too in its own way.

I end this Essay by painting a little picture of quiet, unobtrusive continuity, the sort of continuity that persists in Ulster but is little spoken of – save in derogatory terms of stick-in-the-mud conservatism.

In 1938 when I was slaving as an Assistant Principal – that is to say, an Administrative Cadet in the Ministry of Labour – working on the drafting of Regulations to do with factories and workshops I was called in one day by that incandescent ball of fire, Bill Iliff. (I laugh quietly when I hear otherwise well-informed people talk of dull grey, non-descript civil servants; my career was dominated by a series of colourful characters: Iliff, Scales, Green, Scott Robertson, McKeown, Caldwell, Leitch and a host of others). Iliff dispatched me off to act as clerk to a new body which the Ministry was promoting: a Northern Ireland Council of Social Service. Remember the circumstances: a relatively new Parliament and Government; a new Constitution in the South of Ireland claiming sovereignty over our part of the United Kingdom; and a deep economic depression. I was to serve the N.I.C.S.S. until they had appointed a proper, full-time chief officer. About the only thing I managed to do in my time with them was to help to set this body (which was to become the central, co-ordinating "umbrella" body for countless small voluntary bodies in the social field) on a path of good friendly, working relations with the Government Departments, a situation of mutual trust and respect. I claim no credit, for I could hardly have done anything else, running back and forward every day between Wellington Place and Stormont, getting help here, fitting things together there. Since then I have winced as I watched civil servants in various places similarly seconded to executive bodies, feeling they must show how macho they were to the extent of setting up quite needless distance and tension – all out of fear of being looked on as Yes Men, the silly chumps. Of course it takes two to make a bargain and the readiness of the Stormont Departments to respond and co-operate was essential. They have always enjoyed a well-founded reputation for being easily approached and for having the imagination to foresee the benefits of co-operation with voluntary bodies.

Few things have given me greater pleasure in public life than the knowledge that that sort of good relationship has persisted over more than fifty years now. This is one of the undoubted blessings of the real situation (as distinct from the dreadful image in the Press) that has served the ordinary men and women well and has helped to maintain stability where stability never came easily.

In a major Circular Letter to Local Authorities on the setting up of the new post-war social services issued by the Ministry of Health and Local Government in 1949 after the passing of a new Act of Parliament, the Ministry broke new ground by laying down officially that the success of the local authority would be judged, to some extent, by the way in which it consulted voluntary bodies and carried them with it. This was a big step forward from the authoritarian attitudes that had characterized so much legal and administrative planning everywhere in the British Isles up till then. The Town Clerk of Belfast at the time is reported to have responded: "What do they think we are running? A flower show or something?"

At about the same time the Northern Ireland Council for Social Service decided to set up a proto-type home for old people with a distinctive character and atmosphere to complement the homes then being opened all over the Province by the new Welfare Authorities. They needed a Chairperson, vigorous, fresh, original and uninhibited – and they chose my mother-in-law Muriel Ritson.

Years passed. Muriel went back to England. Others took over. Then one day when the chair fell vacant, the N.I.C.S.S. chose my wife, Stella. She was unlucky in that the Council was beginning to show signs of institutional arthritis and there was less progress than she would have wished to see.

More years passed. Our fourth son Myles was being encouraged at school in the late 1960s to take on some voluntary work outside of school hours. Wisely he eschewed the route chosen by so many of his fellows: tormenting selected old ladies by decorating and re-decorating their kitchens for them every few weeks, it seemed. Instead he joined the N.I.C.S.S. and put in a lot of hard work on their Junior Committee.

One evening in the 1980s our fifth son Quintin telephoned us from Glasgow where he was serving as Welfare Rights Officer under Strathclyde

Regional Council. He wanted to tell us that he had applied for a job in Belfast; and that he had got it. It was with the N.I.C.S.S., now transforming into the N.I.Council for Voluntary Action.

On Just Another Day at the Office

"The out-turn of any piece of Government work is seldom commensurate with the quantity and quality of the civil service input." Thus a Whitehall Permanent Secretary once advised.

Anyone who has seen from the inside a Government Department at work on a big problem will agree that the preparation is prodigious. It is apparent in the brain power invested, the amount of discussion and the conflicting arguments (for no Department is in fact the monolith that it is often said to be). Add the advice of the professional and scientific experts on the staff, the influence of an Advisory Committee, the outcome of negotiations with special interests, the final checking with lawyers, the passage up the ranks of the Department until the Permanent Head is reached before submission to the Minister – the overall total of extended work by some able people is immensely impressive. And yet when the Minister eventually launches his scheme, the quality of the preparation is too often lost sight of, the impact is watered down, the timing is unfortunate, the message does not come across, the thing is a mess.

The preparation may of course not always have been so happy. Often the detail is too elaborate, too many pitfalls foreseen, too many risks guarded against. The advice may have been faulty. The Minister may have been let down. That can all happen.

Who is responsible? Is it the Minister, the named man in the limelight? Or is it the anonymous officials? Under our British system the Minister is responsible and – with some notable exceptions – takes the rap for everything done in his name.

It would be madness to push the question of separating the Minister from his Ministry too far. Much of the working of Government depends precisely on good relations and trust between Ministers and officials, the keeping up of a positive, working continuum. The cases of friction that are known to have occurred have done little good and much harm. Apart from anything else they have been a shameful waste of time.

Stormont from 1921 till 1972 was extremely lucky in that respect for relations were easy and good. Some Ministers were uncommonly successful at getting the best out of their officials. Brian Faulkner was a pleasure to deal with, possibly the model Departmental Minister anywhere. Those Ministers on the extreme right of the Unionist Party were the hardest for officials to get on with and got the least happy response. This was not on account of their views but on account of the way in which they politicized every Departmental issue and suspected every official of deep left-wing tendencies or, worse still, of liberalism.

Ministers walk a tight-rope. Everyone knows that they are served by big Departments and that they are bound to depend on their officials every day of their lives for information and advice. But if you listen closely, you will hardly ever hear them admit that well-known fact. They talk almost exclusively in personal terms: "I have looked closely into this case; I have visited the site myself; I shall pursue the matter personally; and so on." There are two reasons. One is the honourable one of accepting full responsibility; of assuring the public that he is in charge; and of declining to use the Department as an excuse (or, as Sir Wilfred Spender at Stormont used to put it when warning young officials, 'as a lightning conductor'). That would be a sure sign of weakness.

The other reason is perhaps less honourable but wholly understandable: vanity. Politicians love publicity; they need it; they feed on it; they would even buy it. There was the famous case of a Stormont Minister of Education who was invited by the B.B.C. at Ormeau Avenue to talk on radio about some subject not related to his Department. In the course of the visit a B.B.C. man said: "Of course you realize, Minister, that there will be a fee payable for this talk." "How much do I make it out for?" replied the Minister, pulling his cheque book from his jacket pocket. It is amusing now to hear apocryphal versions of that incident transmuted into other places and other times.

Contrary to the superficial nonsense talked about the two Irelands facing each other across a land border of country lanes but never meeting, there were in fact many working contacts between officials in the North and the South on practical matters of common interest and many friendships formed over the years. One incident created some mild fun when a paper on cross-border transport was being prepared jointly by Thekla Beer and Bill Stout. The notable achievement of the Republic in modernizing their Civil Service in the 1960s was much admired in the North and remains the explanation for much of the Republic's success in international affairs. Stormont knew very well the push that Dublin had to make to move from the remnants of "the old Dublin Castle days" (as the fading British regime in Dublin was known) to a modern service on the top-class management lines that have enabled the Republic to play a full part in the United Nations and later in Europe, with effectiveness, dignity and self-respect, as well as keeping up its Embassies and Consulates in many parts of the world – something that Stormont, as a subordinate legislature, lacked and envied. Now-a-days the extraordinary bargain which, as one of the so-called poorer nations, Eire gets from the E.E.C. has been skilfully translated into tangible progress right across the Republic – quietly midwifed by the excellent Dublin civil service.

But they have their troubles, of course, and of a particularly nasty kind. Trust between the Dublin officials and their political masters has been shaken twice – once at the Arms Trial of 1970 and again at the Beef Inquiry in 1992 when evidence of a conflicting nature was publicly tendered. That breach will take time to heal but the signs are that it is the politicians of the older school who are losing the confidence of the public rather than the officials.

How far from the truth of official life and work is the snide accusation that Departmental officials like to have a weak Minister, one whom they can mould to their will and use like putty in their hands, as the critics put it. Any satisfaction along these lines is short-lived, for if the Minister is so weak with his officials he will be weak also in Cabinet, in Parliament, in the Party and in dealing with combative outside interests. And that very soon works to the detriment of the Department.

In many ways the most satisfactory Minister is the one who is hard to persuade, who challenges and questions everything his officials put up to him but who then turns out to be their champion in every outside encounter. Billy Grant, the unlettered shipwright from Duncairn and the Queens Island shipyard, was the supreme example of that type of Minister at Stormont in the 1930s and 1940s, awkward in his office but fearless outside.

Ever since 1921 an odd little quirk lurked in civil service practice at Stormont. When a civil servant sent out an official letter, that letter opened with the standard wording: "I am directed by the *Ministry* of Labour or Finance" (or whatever) whereas in Great Britain the formula ran: "I am directed by the *Minister* of Health or the Home Secretary or His Majesty's Principal Secretary of State" (or whatever the case might be). The distinction was of little importance and few people ever commented on it. The intention was the same in both cases; the outcome was sure to be the same. The Stormont formula arose from an oddity of history. Whereas in England, Wales and Scotland power derived directly from the Sovereign over the centuries, in Northern Ireland (because of the separate administration in Ireland from 1801 till 1921) power devolved to the Ministries indirectly from the expiring office of the Lord Lieutenant of Ireland and thus only indirectly from the Sovereign. Hence the power and authority were surprisingly placed in the Departments rather than in the Ministers.

All very boring, you will think. No one but the present author would take the trouble to dwell on such trivial discrepancies. And yet, and yet, they may be more significant than they appear and may throw a little spark of light on the history of Ulster.

To state openly that the power lay in the Departments could be read as nothing more than an acceptance of reality. Although Stormont Ministers took responsibility for all that was achieved, or not achieved, in their fifty years and must be given the credit as well as the blame, they were frankly only part-timers in a sense, paid nothing more than a derisory allowance. Few public men could have lived, worked and carried out their public duties in the limelight purely on the so-called Ministerial salary.

Besides, the impetus for some nine-tenths of the public business came from the Departments. Besides, again, some like Commerce, Agriculture and Works Branch acted at various times as Agents for Great Britain Departments; for some in turn, British Departments acted as *their* Agents. Once again, some huge fields of work – cash benefits, for example – were (as a matter of firm Government policy) kept strictly in line with the Great Britain rules and regulations. Any wayward deviations would have led to chaos and to injustice to the beneficiaries, it was reckoned. The result was that there was in some Departments little of a political nature for a Minister to do every day within his office. He was better advised to get out and about, selling the policies, explaining them, facing criticisms and bringing back reactions from the public.

Some thoughtful officials in Edinburgh have been wisely thinking ahead on those lines against the day when legislative devolution may come to Scotland.

Let no one dismiss that concept of "public relations" by Ministers as some trivial and unworthy pastime. In a democracy the job of explaining and selling new ideas to the people – the voters and payers – is of crucial importance and is poorly done in England. It is one of the weakest sides of Government work. The undoubted merits of the late lamented Poll Tax in Great Britain were thrown away in the welter of ill-informed criticism: overall fairness in local finance as a whole; the feeling of individual responsibility; and the equality of women. All three were slushed away in the hurry to introduce the new Council Tax which is backward looking, anti-feminist and only superficially fair.

Looking back over the years Unionist Ministers deserved credit in their day for the efforts they made to travel, night after night, often through dangerous republican areas, to explain Departmental policies to the faithful, if thrawn, supporters in remote and dusty Orange Halls. No praise is too great for them when one recalls the great volume of beneficial legislation that they enacted, some of which was not much to their liking, if truth be told, for their stance on most social questions was unionist rather than conservative.

Continuing with the problem of Departments and their Ministers the Stormont Administration was a positive one, pushing ahead, developing proposals, tormenting people with new schemes and so on. The outstanding example was the admirable Ministry of Agriculture, staffed mainly by life-time agriculturalists, many of them scientists converted into administrators, sure of its mission in life, buttressed by some unique arrangements for top-class scientific advice in the University Faculty – and, frankly, pushing on with its work. It had of course the great advantage (which other Ministries envied) that its work was non-political. Party politics scarcely touched it, in contrast with the voluntary church schools in Education, the B Specials in Home Affairs, the location of industry in Commerce and so on. The outcome was that Agriculture felt free to pioneer energetically with marketing schemes, farm improvements, animal health, forestry and a lot else without troubling Ministers at every turn and getting political decisions from them – save again for public relations and debates in the Commons and Senate.

The experience of the Ministry of Agriculture recalls an argument that has run for long in British administration and has not yet been firmly settled. In any British-style Ministry there is a core, a spinal column, so to speak, of generalist, lay administrators who act as the executive force, surrounded by professional and scientific officers whose role, in broad terms, is that of adviser, researcher, inspector, collector of information, contact with the professions, with field workers and so on. The administrator in the course of his career will be moved around from Ministry to Ministry and will acquire a valuable familiarity with all the processes of administration, government and Parliament. He becomes something of an expert in that broader field while remaining, in the eyes of his critics, an amateur at heart, a dilettante on the subject matter of his Departmental field. Part of Britain's failure to modernize and to promote industrial growth is said by some to spring from that very element of amateurism, lack of drive, inability to speak the language of the industrialist or the coal-miner or the farmer. And there is therefore a strong body of informed opinion in favour of specialisation at the heart of the administration – of economists running the Treasury, businessmen running the Board of Trade, school teachers in charge of Education, train drivers, one supposes, at the Ministry of Transport. Those tendencies were given some impetus by the Fulton Reforms of the late 1960s when the civil service was urged to move from generalist amateurism to specialized professionalism. An officer, it was argued, should devote his career to one field of work, say Home Office, Police and Prisons; or Industry, Power and Transport; or the Social

Services; and become a recognized specialist so as to provide knowledge and continuity, able to talk convincingly to outside interests. Something approaching the German system, perhaps, with Herr Doktors and Frau Doktors at every turn. Those arguments were attractive and the long-standing example of the Stormont Ministry of Agriculture supported them; so also did the Stormont Ministry of Education where professional educationists were repeatedly promoted to top administrative positions. The arguments against the idea are of course that the specialist tends to concentrate purely on his speciality, to have little sensitivity for other interests and to finish up pushing his own empire in a situation where one hand of Government doesn't know what the other hand is doing – along the very same corridor perhaps.

Energy and drive by specialists have to be constantly weighed against the value of steadiness, wisdom and overall stability. One small but clear example of the value to a country of a wise "amateur" administration was to be seen in Rhodesia in the 1970s and 1980s where a most admirable civil service kept pegging away, under a series of differing political bosses through colonial status, U.D.I. to Independence, day by day, yet keeping the ship on an even keel in some extraordinarily rough waters. One of their top men was an old Post Office hand, still speaking with a County Londonderry accent, responsible for the free and fair election machinery that stood up to enormous strains. It is hard to see how specialists could have done any better.

Another, more promising, way ahead was pointed in the early 1970s by Liam Devlin in Dublin, a leading shipping executive brought in to advise on modernizing the Republic's administrative structure.

Devlin, a clear-headed pragmatist, went straight for what he saw as the nub of the matter, the congestion at the heart of the system.

Ministers and senior officials had become over-laden with far too much detailed executive work at the same time as they were supposed to be thinking ahead and devising policy. And he was also impatient with the pretence of Ministers standing up in the Dail trying to answer questions on detail across the country which, in all conscience, they could not possibly be expected to know about, let alone control.

His advice was simple: let the Minister, with a small Headquarters office, answer only for what he can reasonably be expected to know and to control: legislation, policy, finance and priorities; then hive off all the subordinate executive and clerical work to a new Agency equipped for that job and working under Guide Lines. The Minister and his top officials would thus be freed from the burden of detail and the incubus of constitutional make-believe; the Agency would be free to get on with serving the public and liberated from the need to keep looking over its shoulder and answering "damn-silly queries" from Headquarters or as Liam Devlin put it to me personally one evening in Belfast: the chaps will now be free to look outwards (into the community) rather than always upwards (to the politicians)

It is now interesting to see Whitehall moving briskly along the same lines under its derivative programme: "Next Steps", hiving off the Passport Office, the Vehicle Licensing Office, Cash Benefits and so on to executive agencies. It will be rewarding to see a plaque put up in Downing Street in honour of Liam Devlin who led the way.

On a small matter of little importance compared with the big issues dealt with in this essay, may I mention that I had not been employed very long in an office before I realized that some good work fell short simply because it was poorly presented. Colleagues would produce memoranda that were better informed, more closely reasoned and no doubt wiser than mine; but they sometimes cast them in such a dense, unrelieved form that they failed to make the impact they deserved with Ministers, M.P.s, outside interests and so on. I quickly learned the simple trick of breaking up a memo with short paragraphs, occasional short sentences and the use of capital letters to introduce, and stress, important concepts. As well as that, I always aimed to use Plain Words if I could.

I still favour the use of capital letters out of adherence to a principle which I always held and which I hold even more firmly to-day: the principle of respect for authority and for those exercising authority: Parliament, Acts of Parliament, the Statute Book, the Judiciary, Consultants, Doctors, Councillors and so on. I do not share the modern habit of constantly denigrating authority, of undermining respect and of pulling everything down to the lowest common level. I know very well that this is sincerely believed to reflect aspects of modern democracy and egalitarianism. But I don't like it. I think it bad. And so I still persist – for what it is worth – in dignifying authority with capital letters as a tiny contribution to respect and stability, a token if nothing else. The trouble is that I overdo it unless an Editor stops me.

In a quite different sense I have all my working life favoured the use of "ize" rather than "ise": emphasize, philosophize, realize, recognize and so on. This was partly out of regard for etymology and partly for the sake of style. My practice has often been criticized; but I do not mind. I need only point to the Shorter Oxford English Dictionary for overwhelming support, not to mention Fowler and, especially, Partridge in his Usage and Abusage.

In another attempt at lifting up this dreary subject, let us turn to the great Russian novelist Leo Tolstoy. Lecturing us from the heights of nineteenth century literature, philosophy and military science Tolstoy shows us in "War and Peace" the leaders of society as corks on top of the water, carried endlessly to and fro on the tide of events. Again and again he projects Army chiefs in those splendid white uniforms of theirs, strutting up and down through the mud, persuading themselves that they were in charge of events when in fact huge forces were at work across Europe that they could not control, still less arrest: national pride, personal ambition, trade, greed, lust, the terrain, the climate. Even the admirable Czar Alexander the First could do little. Even the redoubtable Napoleon comes out in practice as nothing like the military genius of the orthodox history books.

It would strengthen democracy and help to restore the good name of politicians, now sadly in decline, if present-day Ministers were to admit from time to time that there are tides which they cannot control.

On Getting to know the Great Essayist William Haslett

So you think I have made a careless mistake in mis-spelling the name of this giant of English letters? Just wait a moment.

When, on making good some gaps in my knowledge of English literature, I came to read William Hazlitt, 1778 to 1830, I enjoyed his Essays enormously. First, there were so many of them. Next, they were so varied. Then, they were so easy to read. Above all, they were so spirited: he had such strong views, such likes and dislikes, such hates and loves. Here was a writer after my own heart – and I do not make that claim lightly, as you will see.

At one moment you are deep in literary criticism, as for example in the very first sentence of Hazlitt's Lectures on the Comic Writers: "Man is the only animal that laughs and weeps; for he is the only animal that is struck with the difference between what things are and what they ought to be." The next moment you are at a prize-fight, not just as an impartial onlooker but as a fervent partisan, for boxing was one of Hazlitt's passions; and I am amused to find that his favourite pugilist was a certain Tom Oliver. A few minutes later you are setting off on a journey with Hazlitt: "One of the pleasantest things in the world is going on a journey; but I like to go by myself . . . I am never less alone than when alone." Exactly how I feel. He is one of the few accomplished writers who let you into the secrets of his skill: "It is not easy to write a familiar style . . . there is nothing that requires more precision and, if I may say so, purity of expression." Writing? Yes but that is not all. Hazlitt is a competent painter as well and once again lets you into some of the secrets of that occupation: "There is a pleasure in painting that none but painters know. In writing, you have to contend with the world; in painting, you have only to carry on a friendly strife with nature. You sit down to your task, and are happy."

His further advice on painting tells us much about the man himself. Having failed to reach the heights of success with his painting: "I flung away my pencil in disgust and despair," he tells us. "Otherwise I might have done as well as others, I dare say, but for a desire to do too well." How I sympathize.

It is perhaps in his theatre criticisms that Hazlitt's likes and dislikes begin to show most clearly. His analysis of the dramatic power and skill of the Mrs.Siddons he admired so much is stunning: "She produced the most overpowering effects without the slightest effort, by a look, a word, a gesture. Can I ever forget the slight pause she made, as Lady Macbeth reading the letter: 'When I demanded to know more of them, they made themselves into air' (sic) . . . the glance at which you could feel the audience quiver and cower."

When Edmund Kean was hooted from the stage in 1814 by a lot of vulgar hoodlums: "The vulgar in their inmost souls admire nothing but the vulgar; the commonplace nothing but the commonplace; the superficial nothing but the superficial." What a champion to have! How it would sustain a Chancellor of the Exchequer to-day, an Archbishop, an Heir to the Throne to have the warm support and brilliant advocacy of a William Hazlitt.

On a totally different plane of admiration and support are Hazlitt's moving tributes to his own father, a poor Preacher who eked out his meagre income by taking pupils for private tuition. Not only does William present his father as a conscientious scholar and teacher but as a man of "stainless integrity." So much so indeed that William once heard "a shrewd man say he would never send a son of his to my father lest the boy should be so schooled in truth as to be disqualified from getting his living in the world." Knowing something, now, of the restless life William Hazlitt senior led, I am all the more impressed by the devotion touchingly shown by the son, the author, the writer.

For a writer he was, above all else. As R.L.Stevenson declared, some fifty years after Hazlitt's death; "We are mighty fine fellows, but we cannot write like William Hazlitt." It is important to grasp that truth before we dig any further.

Let us turn now to Robert Lynd for some closer guidance. In one of his most guileless yet penetrating essays Lynd warns us: "Hazlitt was not born to good fortune . . . he was the possessor of a demon that fought against his happiness . . . He separated from both the women he married and seems to have quarrelled at some time or other with all his friends." Those comments are fully borne out by several of his talented friends. Coleridge, for example: "he has a jealous, gloomy and an irritable pride." Leigh Hunt thought that "I should have a still greater affection for him if he would let me; but I declare to God I never seem to know whether he is pleased or displeased, cordial or uncordial – indeed his manners are never cordial". Even Lamb, the gentlest of men, thought Hazlitt "to be . . . one of the wisest and finest spirits breathing" but was forced to add "in his natural state" warning us of Hazlitt's unnatural state, the darker side. And Robert Lynd tellingly interprets Hazlitt's writings with the explanation: "the sun shines on the past oftener than on the present or future".

The human side of Hazlitt's tortured life shows up in his many passionate love-affairs. He seems to have been perpetually in love with some woman or other. His close friend Peter George Patmore, father of the poet Coventry Patmore, has alleged that he never knew Hazlitt but he was in love. Indeed one of Hazlitt's more passionate outbursts occurs in a letter written to Patmore on 31st May 1822 from Edinburgh where, and while, Hazlitt was pursuing his divorce suit in the Scottish Consistory Courts, then more amenable on those matters apparently than the English Courts. I came upon this letter in a charming volume "The Faber Book of Letters." Here William lets himself go in recounting ungraciously his vigorous, impetuous wooing of the Landlord's daughter, Sarah Walker: "a regular lodging-house decoy . . . she has an itch for being slabbered and felt . . . letting me enjoy her through her petticoats . . . admitting all sorts of indecent liberties . . . do not let any one else do so, he said to her, no not now, was her answer, that is [simply] because there was nobody in the house to do it with her . . . the bitch wants a stallion and hates a lover . . ." Very understandably Sarah found all this too much to take and walked away, which was lucky for me as my delicate sensibilities could scarcely have borne any more of Hazlitt's behaviour. There is much more of the same in Hazlitt's "Liber Amoris".

So, where does this leave William Hazlitt in the end? Christopher Salvesen sums up the man: "The best prose writer of his age . . . Unfortunately the master essayist also achieved a reputation as a scoundrel, an adulterer, a drunk; and when death came to him on 18th September 1830 he was friendless, penniless and living in a London slum." Other scholars may have sought to qualify that description of his end and to argue that circumstances were not quite so bad; but a vivid picture remains, in all its essentials, of a brilliant mind imprisoned in an awkward, fractured personality. A thrawn fellow, as we say.

Having steeped myself in Hazlitt's writings I then began to ask where he came from and when: the questions of history and geography which need to be answered in any full appreciation of a great man's achievement.

Anthologists, editors, commentators, one after another record "from Tipperary", "the son of a non-conformist clergyman in Tipperary" and leave it at that, obviously relying on the findings of the editor or commentator who went before them and not wanting to delve too deeply into Irish affairs.

I was not satisfied. Tipperary did not seem to me to be the likeliest origin for a Hazlitt. There have been a few Hazlitts in that county but not many and not significant.

In North Antrim and North Derry Hazlitts abound. They have been around in large numbers for centuries. As you drive along the main road in the Castlerock area you pass the Londonderry County Education Authority school, clearly marked: The Hezlitt School. And the County would hardly name one of its schools after a family without good reason. The Chief Clerk to the Coleraine Rural District Council was, for long, a Haslett. One of the Royal Navy's supreme Submariners was Vice-Admiral A.R.Hezlet of Aghadowey son of Major General Hezlet and author of the history of the "B Specials". My own direct family can boast of a strong Haslett connection in the Roe Valley, first at Drumneecy, then Ballyleighery and ultimately at Dernaflaw and Derryork. Here we had the epitome of the Ulster-Scot tradition, small farmers, tenant farmers, immensely frugal and hard-working, the strictest of Presbyterians. Two of them, Uncle Bob and Uncle Alec, went into the stone-mason business and won contracts, single-handed, for installing marble panelling at the Kelvin Hall in Glasgow and (in the eyes of every Belfastman) at that even more prestigious edifice, the ornate Belfast City Hall when it was being put up in the first few years of this century. And it was a delight one morning a year or two ago, to hear their direct descendant Malcolm Haslett of the B.B.C. World Service, reading and translating from the Russian newspapers with Brian Redhead in Moscow.

I was also struck by the Christian names favoured by the family of William Hazlitt, both before and after his time: William, John, William, John. The genealogist knows to place some weight on such a distinctive pattern of names. If the pattern had run: Jasper, Rupert, Jasper, Rupert – I should have paid little attention; but the close similarity to the pattern of Christian names I knew so well in County Derry right down to the present day made me think.

Then there is the factual matter of his father's theological training. Hazlitt tells us in plain words that his father had been sent by his parents to the University of Glasgow to prepare for the Presbyterian ministry – a picture familiar in every Presbyterian home in Antrim and Derry whence the Scottish coast can be seen on a clear day. The local legends often have the added poignancy of a description of the tub of butter in the student's luggage to help pay for his lodgings. Altogether rather more an Ulster connection, one would think, than a Munster one.

There remains, you may argue, the stumbling block of the disparity in the spelling of the family name itself: Hazlett, Hezlet, Haslett and so on. Not so. I have learned to disregard small discrepancies in the recording of family names in the earlier centuries. Not until compulsory registration of births, deaths and marriages had been established during the nineteenth century, followed shortly by compulsory universal education, did the spelling of names become to any degree standardized. I have noted down countless discrepancies on headstones side by side recording, from the same townland and on the same grave, a Douglass and a Douglas, a Fleming and a Flemming, a Dunseith and a Dunceith, a Ray and a Wray. After having anguished in the early years of my work on family history over such differences, and after having puzzled over their possible significance, I learned to put the whole problem in perspective. I now openly dismiss it. I have proven the point far beyond any argument by recording, elsewhere, no fewer than twelve variants in the spelling of one of my family names: Morell, Morrell, Murial etc. and fully as many in the spelling of Shearer, Sherrard, Sherer, Shirer and so on. So: the little matter of an 's' or a 'z' in these findings of the Haslett clan are of no importance.

On looking up my own Notes recently I was further encouraged by finding one of our own Hasletts of Dernaflaw commemorated on a headstone as "Hazlett" with two daughters bearing the lovely names of Letitia and Hadessa.

All these observations and conclusions pointed me, independently, in the direction of a North Ulster origin for William Hazlitt.

Turning to the Dictionary of National Biography, that work of "stainless integrity" (if I may use Hazlitt's own phrase), I found the firm statement: "William Hazlitt, son of William grandson of John, originally of County Antrim". That re-inforced the pattern I was beginning to trace; and did so with great authority.

Then running through the various published "lives" of Hazlitt, I at last came upon the definitive story. It is by that most perceptive writer and student of Irish affairs, the Rt.Hon.Augustine Birrell.

Tradition tells us, he writes, of Hazlitts or Hasletts to be found in Antrim and in Coleraine and other parts of the North of Ireland. They were Protestants, "though affecting the Presbyterian colour" (an odd phrase to choose for such a stern attachment). One of them, a John Haslett was a flax merchant – where better to deal in flax in the eighteenth century than in Antrim and Derry? – recorded around 1735. Eventually he grew rich and went off to set up business at Shrone Hill, County Tipperary. Some descendants of his still (Birrell was writing in 1902) live in the Tipperary region. Other Hasletts, needless to say, emigrated to America, notably a Col.John Haslett of the Coleraine branch of the family. Augustine Birrell's work bears all the hallmarks of careful, original research and gives much relevant detail. I feel justified in relying on Birrell as he was a Barrister, a Bencher, a Professor of Law and the author of several substantial works. Knowing something of the unhappy end to his career, as Chief Secretary in Ireland under the British Crown at the time of the 1916 Rebellion, we may reasonably wish – as he may well have wished himself – that he had stuck to biography and literature.

Although I have not found any Hasletts in the records of the main Plantation of Ulster under King James the First in the earliest years of the 1600s, I see them as part of the flood of Scottish Presbyterians who kept coming over to Ulster in successive waves during the seventeenth century and forming an integral, recognizable, recorded part of the Ulster-Scot tradition. I was pleased, the other day, to find among my own Notes a firmly authenticated reference to a Hazlitt attending First Dunboe Church (Castlerock) in 1663 along with – and this is significant – other undoubted immigrants from Southern Scotland: Fulton, Morrison, Oliver and so on. Little does it matter which combination of 's' or 'z', 'e', or 'i' a tired clergyman or his clerk may have thrown together on the church register, any wet, cold day after a baptism, a marriage or a funeral and by the poor light of a dim oil lamp.

In these matters I always do what I can to try to trace the Ulster-Scot settlers back to their undoubted origins in Scotland, a lonely, thankless task to which I have devoted my single-handed efforts for many years now. For William Haslett I can firmly cite: "John Heslett (an old spelling of Haslett or Hazlitt) waulker, burgess of Glasgow, 1575". Here I am quoting verbatim from the greatest authority on Scottish names, G.F.Black.

And similarly down to the present times. One of my best friends in life has been William Haslett of County Derry, my first cousin, an unusual man of many parts – farmer, teacher, philosopher, seeker after abstruse religions, and above all enviable collector of colleagues, neighbours, cronies, oddities, professors, visitors and unsuspecting hosts. Is it any wonder that I claim both William Haslett and William Haslett as my kinsmen? Let me repeat some lines I wrote in an obituary notice for one of these cousins in 1992:

A bunch of friends, college mates, professional colleagues, neighbours were the hall-mark of William Haslett's long, varied and surprising life. But the point is that they had a reality and an importance far beyond the scope of mere ceilidh and gossip. They sustained him loyally during his later years of acute pain and confinement. They made it possible for Leslie and him to go on living in what might seem, to the uninformed, the isolation of Whitehead, County Antrim. And as final proof of their affection and devotion they were all there to support Leslie and the family at one of the most impressive cremation funerals in modern Ulster, that Wednesday in January 1992.

All in all, and taking the genealogical liberties which any searcher in the field of family history in Ireland is entitled to allow himself, I take my stand on the belief that William Haslett, one of the greatest essayists in the English language, was indeed my distant cousin and an Ulsterman.

On Managing the Grammar Schools

I smile quietly to myself as I listen to all those stories of the terrible pressure now-a-days on the managers of secondary schools in England and Wales. Poor things. How I pity them. Local Management of Schools? What a burden! More resources must obviously be rushed to the schools. Own budgets? What an imposition! The poor oppressed Heads there are going to need a big rise in pay.

The voluntary grammar schools, as part of the whole education system in Ulster, fought those battles away back more than forty years ago and emerged with a system that satisfied them, satisfied the Government and most certainly satisfied the parents. Local management became the general rule for most grammar schools. Budgets became their bread and butter.

Not content with that, they gained acceptance for a further refinement in which the A schools received direct Government grants towards capital works and the B schools kept aloof to the extent of doing without. Yet all of them, fifty-seven last time I counted them, stayed within the overall state system, abided by the Ministry's Regulations and accepted inspection by the Ministry's Inspectors. In some ways they helped to set the standards and the pace of the whole system. They managed to reach the status of truly voluntary bodies fully within the state education system. In a real sense it could be said that in 1948 they were opting in rather than opting out.

My mention here of inspection by higher authority is no mere pious reference, for I believe strongly in the value for all concerned of rigorous, independent inspection. I look on it as one of the great losses of our time – comparable in a quite different field with the disappearance of the Medical Officer of Health – that inspection has been so bad-mouthed and so down-graded in the modern systems of sophisticated management. Each time one of those British disasters or administrative scandals occurs and people are killed or made to suffer unbearably I quietly ask the three questions: "What were the bosses doing all this time? Did they not know what was going on? When did they last inspect?"

The grammar school arrangements were negotiated and then monitored by a hard-working but self-effacing body, the Association of Governing Bodies of Grammar Schools in Northern Ireland. And let us be clear: Catholic Schools, Protestant Schools, non-sectarian schools – all took part, side by side.

They had a common interest. That was what bound them together. The common interest was far stronger than the few features which might have divided them. And so the Association succeeded. That was the secret – along with sheer hard work.

On the admission of pupils and the payment for pupils another success was scored in the 1940s in the form of a pioneering type of voucher system, whereby each child that qualified for a grammar school had his or her fees paid by the State at the school of his or her choice, subject only to the payment by the parent of a small, tightly controlled capital fee, starting in 1948 at as low a figure as three pounds a year! Needless to say all those matters have been argued over, changed and developed many times since 1948. Some of them still give headaches; but the system works; and the parents love it.

One of my objects in setting out all those tiresome administrative arrangements here in this Essay is to show that a good, modern and by now proven system had been devised in Ulster forty years before the big changes of the late 1980s were even dreamed of in England and to show that there was ample working experience available within the United Kingdom to be studied by English politicians, managers and heads. Many points were common to both areas, some were different, some better here, some worse there – but overall the Ulster experience was most telling and highly relevant. So far as I know it remained unused, untapped, ignored. Or was it followed?

But the Ulster people have a far deeper satisfaction than the flattery that now comes from being imitated, the satisfaction of knowing that their grammar schools are amongst the best in the British Isles and that their examination results stand high in the league – suddenly becoming popular in England – of G.C.E. A levels, with some Ulster schools achieving remarkable placings.

Though partly due to the admirable system, partly to the dedicated teachers and partly to the selection of pupils, those achievements can be traced to yet another cause. The pupils want to learn. When Strathearn School for Girls on the Belmont Road in East Belfast topped some British results a few years ago, the Headmistress, Miss Lamb, modestly said on B.B.C. Radio Four: "We have no problems with discipline here. The girls want to learn. They want to do well. They want to get on. We can therefore give all our time to teaching, from Monday morning till Friday evening".

Oxford and Cambridge Admission Tutors know those facts and not only accept but go out and look for students from the Ulster Grammar Schools. College lists that used to feature Campbell, Methody, Academy and Inst now glow with names from Dominican College, Regent House, Rainey, Thornhill, Ballymena Academy, Coleraine Inst and so on, a source of immense satisfaction all round. No wonder Ulster parents are not only proud but fiercely protective of their excellent schools. Perhaps that thought might be kept in mind next time Ulster people are denounced as intransigeant and unbending and tardy in taking up the latest trends.

Much of the credit for good teaching in these excellent schools must go to the main State Teacher Training establishment, Stranmillis College in Belfast. There, dedicated lecturers and tutors kept their heads during the Sixties and Seventies, rejecting many of the fads of those times, the sillier theories and practices. The outcome was seen in generation after generation of young teachers, well trained in the basics but also taught to beware of fanciful whims; and those influences made themselves felt right up through the school system. We owe much more to Stranmillis than merely a continuous supply of teachers; we owe to Stranmillis a solid body of sound teaching practice that has proven its value again and again. Ulster and indeed the United Kingdom have every reason to be grateful and to acknowledge the debt we all owe.

The grammar schools have not had an easy run by any means. In the 1970s they had to fight for their very existence when Direct Rule Ministers made a heavy-handed attempt to impose comprehensive schools on the Province without any mandate – political, electoral or popular. Luckily the Direct Rule

Minister in charge was so unfortunate that he came a cropper. When I tackled him face to face one day and asked him the straight question: "Why have you consulted many different bodies about the abolition of the grammar schools and never consulted the Governing Bodies Association?" he replied to our astonishment: "Because I knew what you would say". Such political naivete was bound to bring down both the Minister and his programme. We were not opposing comprehensive schools. We were not speaking against them. As sensible, practical people we recognized that there were times and situations when a comprehensive school was the right answer to a community's needs. And we had set out our views, with closely argued detail, in a booklet deliberately entitled: "Witness for Worth." What we were objecting to was the needless destruction on doctrinaire grounds (and without a mandate) of a whole system of grammar schools – voluntary and state, to be clear – beloved by the people and warmly supported by the parents. Our view carried. Reason won the day.

But there was a deeper issue at stake. Not only was there an attack being mounted against the grammar schools based on the politics of envy and greed, but those schools were being set against the intermediate schools, set against them in a quite unnecessary dichotomy and even conflict. We looked on that horrid "two-camp" approach as fundamentally bad. We wanted to see variety in a diversified system and in May 1978 went so far as to devise the aim: – not of a system of comprehensive schools, but a comprehensive system of secondary schools, "an all-embracing system that is wide enough and flexible enough to contain a variety of different types of school all designed to cater for the spiritual, moral, mental and physical development of different children in the different areas and districts". We were encouraged to note that the Ministry of Education adopted that formula shortly afterwards in an official document. Not a bad proposal. Indeed looking back now, from 1994 in the United Kingdom as a whole, it was surely a remarkably far-seeing and perceptive contribution to educational thinking – in May 1978.

In my time – the 1950s, 1960s and 1970s – the stance of the Catholic grammar schools differed from that of the Protestant and non-denominational schools in one or two interesting ways. One was that they were represented by teacher-governors rather than by lay governors whereas the Protestant, non-denominational and state schools were governed by non-teacher lay men and women. It had long been their system to appoint as chairman of governors of one school the clerical teaching head of a neighbouring school; and he or she naturally then came to the fore as the school's representative. There were advantages. Those men and women, though sitting alongside us as governors in consultation, knew so much more about teaching that they were able to educate us around the table. Brother Murphy, Rev.Dr.Farren, Sister Laurentia taught us a lot. But the drawback was the corresponding failure to bring forward more Catholic lay men to take part in public life – and, even more strikingly, Catholic lay women in those years.

The other deeply rooted attitude was the respect in which the Catholic schools held the local Ministry of Education at Stormont – or latterly at Rathgael – and the harmonious and trusting relationship which they enjoyed. When speaking at public functions I used to warn people, light-heartedly, that when visiting the Ministry of Education they should take care not to be trampled under foot by the forward rush of clerical heads and managers along the corridors of power. That attitude of the Catholic schools towards the Ministry once came to a crunch when the Governing Bodies were setting out to belabour the Ministry itself in the battle about enforced comprehensive schools. The Protestant schools would have gone bare-knuckled for those so-and-sos in the Ministry; it was the Catholic schools that held them back.

That was no isolated incident. It represents a long-standing trust and working relationship. And it runs very deep. The political leaders of the nationalist community in Ulster know all this far better than I do, but I dearly wish they would stand up and say so – in other words, break out of the negative stance and admit positively how well their schools have been treated since 1921 and how happy relationships have been between the managers of the Catholic voluntary schools and the Stormont administration over the generations. Once in a while a Bishop, opening a small school somewhere, does express his satisfaction but that does not take us very far. What is needed is for the political leaders of the nationalist community to come out of the closet and admit publicly that many aspects of Ulster administration have served their people well – schools, colleges, universities, health, commerce, social security, agriculture, the civil service and, yes, the police. It ought not to be left to an anonymous nobody like me to speak up on these matters as I do repeatedly and unreservedly – most recently in a long and exceptionally dreary article in the learned London journal: "Contemporary Record." One wise word from John Hume at Westminster or one telling phrase from Seamus Mallon on television would do far more good to start to get us all away from the negative culture of grievance which the Nationalists, I am sorry to say, have assiduously cultivated since 1921. I know as well as anyone that they have their objections, their disappointments, their downright criticisms. Of course they have. Which of us hasn't? But those are as nothing when set against the undoubted, long-term benefits of the Stormont system to the Catholic community over seventy years.

My constant emphasis on grammar schools may carry a suggestion of old-fashioned adherence to traditional 'academic' subjects and of a school population pathetically clinging to Greek and Latin. Any such suggestion would be wildly out of date and far from reality. Hardly any pupils do Greek now and few do Latin. The curriculum has long ago moved on to economics, computer science, social studies, craft, design and technology. And it will move further in that direction. What matters, deep down, is the teacher and the taught, the quality of the teaching, the keenness of the pupils, the support of the parents, the emphasis on learning for its own sake, the respect for books, the richness of "the other curriculum", the readiness of the teachers to work outside school hours and the readiness of the pupils to push them to do so.

I take it on myself to invert Francis Bacon's celebrated and once seminal phrase "the science of grammar" to "the grammar of science" as one of the key-notes of modern grammar school teaching.

Just wait till I tell you what I mean.

One evening at a public dinner in Belfast Professor Robert Matthew, the great British architect and town planner, was the guest speaker. It was snowing and terribly cold. Robert was telling us about the creation of the first chair in architecture at that allegedly staid and conservative institution, Edinburgh University, and was conveying the reaction of the old men in the

Senior Common Room. "What? a chair in architecture? That's not a University subject! Not academic! What will they be doing next? A chair in plumbing? Ha! Ha!" Professor Robert Matthew had only to point to the iced-up windows, to the intense cold and to the feeble heating: "A chair in plumbing? Why not? What better?" to evoke a big round of applause.

I look forward to seeing grammar school boys and girls studying the history and practice of plumbing or of irrigating the deserts from the oceans or keeping fresh and clean our lovely rivers and lakes. The grammar of science.

On Making Good the gaps in an Ulsterman's knowledge of English Literature

Having spent the first sixty-five years of my life in Ulster I knew that there were glaring gaps in my knowledge of English literature. But it was not until I did a sort of stock-taking a few years ago that I came to see how big those gaps were and how serious.

At school in Belfast in the 1920s we had been given a good grounding and we came away with a fair picture of the great novelists, the essayists and the short story writers, a close acquaintance with Shakespeare and a first hand familiarity with the lyric poets. Of all those the novelists meant least for as young boys few of us had the experience of life, the maturity and the insight to grasp the depth and subtlety of character and motivation. What for example could any ordinary schoolboy take away from George Meredith's "Lord Ormont" or "The Amazing Marriage" which we read in the Fifth Form?

I now believe that girls of the same age got more from the classic novels than boys did but it is my own shortcomings that I am dealing with here. And why make them look still worse by comparison?

Studying French and German at University under Professor Savory and Professor Waterhouse I had a much more orderly and comprehensive approach to the literature in both those languages – and correspondingly less time for reading English.

As an Irishman living in Ireland I absorbed automatically the great line of Anglo-Irish writers from Jonathan Swift to Shaw, Wilde, Yeats, Joyce, O'Casey, O'Connor and others through all sorts of channels including, away above anything else in my memory, Michael McLiammoir's one-man show "The Importance of Being Oscar", a supreme performance at the Belfast Opera House in the last year of that great actor's career. We were lucky to have been there. For once we can say with literal truth that we shall not see his like again.

Once I had passed the age of seventy I firmly decided to drop all those committee memberships and continuing responsibilities to voluntary social and educational work that I had carried, without a break, for fifty years since 1932. I was determined to make way for younger people with new ideas and in touch with the rising generation; and to make way, in another sense, for doing those things in my private life that I knew I had neglected.

Although many an evangelical preacher in a Mission Tent had bawled at us about the famous characters in Bunyan's "Pilgrim's Progress" I was ashamed to say that I had never actually read the whole of that work straight through. Nor had I ever sat down and read Alexander Pope, even though I had often heard my own voice bringing off some of his famous lines in the office at Stormont: "Some praise at morning what they blame at night but always think the last opinion right". Like everyone else, it seems, I had read Pope but had never actually been seen reading him.

Francis Bacon and Ben Jonson – which was which? Did Bacon really write the poems and plays attributed to Jonson? or was it vice-versa? When did Piers the Plowman live and write? Was Arnold Bennett a great writer or merely a superficial journalist? Oh, and Aphra Behn. I had long been puzzled: a man or a woman? English or foreign? So I set myself the task of filling in those gaps and satisfying my curiosity once and for all in a planned programme.

Piers the Plowman is of course the character, not the author. That was William Langland, writing in Middle English language around 1360 till 1400 or so; Piers was Everyman on a pilgrimage to salvation in a dream told in an allegorical poem of great beauty, wit and power. Along with "The Canterbury Tales" it must rank as one of the foundations of our literature. I was delighted with Langland's use of alliteration in such a soft, intimate and beguiling way: "The Fair Field Full of Folk found I there bytwene . . . In a Somer Seson when soft was the sonne . . . I shope me into shrouds as I a shep were" – and so on, endlessly fascinating to my ear.

Sir Francis Bacon, Lord Verulam, Viscount St.Albans, Lord Chancellor of England captivated me entirely. Enormously intelligent with wide scientific interests as well as legal, literary and philosophical interests he was far ahead of his time. He lived a life that struck me as, at one and the same time, brilliant and tragic. What sadder decline for a distinguished Lord Chancellor than to be charged by his own Lord Chief Justice with accepting bribes – and to be forced to admit the factual truth of that charge. Still, a shining star in our sky and the author of Essays so full of learning, wisdom and prescience that they require you to read them several times over. "I have taken all knowledge to be my province", as Francis Bacon said when he was just thirty years of age.

Ben Jonson stemmed originally from Annan in Southern Scotland, the homeland of the Johnsons who came to people Ulster so prolifically in the seventeenth century. Johnson is still one of the commonest names in Ulster to-day, however it is spelt, and I long ago gave up any fussy concern over the detail of name-spelling at any time up till the middle of the nineteenth century or thereabouts. It is intriguing to see how often people in the complex and crowded Britain at any epoch can be quickly traced back to their local roots.

Personally – in spite of all that – I found it hard to get close to Ben Jonson, a severe classicist who looked on his near contemporary, that actor-manager fellow William Shakespeare, as a rough unlettered hack.

His own great output of highly polished plays, poems, essays and above all masques (so popular in the reigns of James I and Charles I) have much less appeal now than when they were being written and produced. He must have enjoyed a big following in his day, a following sufficient to cause a certain Jack Young, passing by his gravestone in Westminster Abbey, to give a stonemason eighteen pence to add the simple but stunning inscription: "O Rare Ben Jonson". He did redeem himself in our eyes eventually by writing of Shakespeare – reluctantly and none too graciously: "there was ever more in him to be praised than to be pardoned". And we in turn must forgive Ben Jonson everything on account of his immortal lines:

"Drink to me only with thine eyes . . ."

As women featured so little in English letters before Fanny Burney and Jane Austen the achievements of Aphra Behn are impressive. She is thought to have written no fewer than eighteen plays for the theatre in the years around 1670 to 1690, many prose romances and a number of occasional poems. None, alas, are playable or enjoyable to-day. Still, she won enough fame in her time to be given the honour of a burial in the Abbey.

An ordinary enough story, you may think. But just wait another minute. After the Restoration England's great rival was the Netherlands with whom we were constantly at war. The sound of their guns could be heard in the City of London in 1667, when they had the nerve to sail up the Thames. King Charles the Second felt that he needed a secret agent to be planted in Antwerp. Whom did he choose? A woman. An Englishwoman, Aphra, born Amis, and married to a city merchant, Behn, of Dutch extraction.

Getting to grips with the eighteenth century novelists – Richardson, Sterne (another Irishman), Fielding and Smollett – took up an awful lot of my time. They were so wordy. Richardson's "Clarissa" in 1747 and 1748, for example, with its one million words, occupied me for a whole month of hard reading, almost (but not quite) driving me to commit the sin of sitting down to read a novel before mid-day.

To go back a step. Although Richardson and the others are generally taken to be the fathers of the English novel, I myself must place Daniel Defoe's "Moll Flanders" well ahead of them both in time and in sheer influence. Defoe seems to have been a prodigious worker in many fields. "Moll" which came out in 1722 is racy, readable and (in spite of some extraordinary ups and downs in Moll's much married life) believable and sympathetic. I read it twice.

My father had always been a devoted reader of Sir Walter Scott, who has remained popular and well regarded in Ulster-Scot circles in Ulster. I can recall my father setting off in the 1920s on a pilgrimage from Ballynafeigh to Abbotsford, to do homage to the great man. I had therefore read many of Scott's novels in my youth, under my father's stimulating influence, but I had retained little. I therefore sat down, as part of this sedentary Odyssey, and read one after the other three of his best: Guy Mannering, Old Mortality and The Antiquary. I loved them all with their good stories, their memorable characters and their wealth of well-researched historical detail. I also enjoyed the valuable Author's Notes which Scott often added. This last feature yielded a double dividend by re-inforcing and extending the lore I had been picking up in the course of my laborious studies into family history in Southern Scotland.

On top of all the merits of the Scott novels I have been deeply impressed by the energy and output of the man. Between 1810 and 1830 he seemed to be producing a hefty volume every six months or so – on top of his substantial legal duties as Sheriff of Selkirk and his unfortunate business affairs in Edinburgh and his translations of Goethe from the German and his physical disability stemming from infantile paralysis and his strenuous travels around the countryside collecting Border Ballads and preserving them for us. A remarkable man. And, like Robbie Burns, James Hogg, David Hume and so many others he flourished after – and possibly because of – the Union of the two Parliaments in 1707.

What exactly was William Blake – an artist or an engraver or a visionary or a poet or a revolutionary or a madman or a workaholic or a Christian apologist? He was all of those things. In some lights a towering poet fit to stand alongside

Chaucer, Shakespeare and Milton; in other lights a pathetic figure working away at his intricate engravings even when he was seriously ill in the 1820s. To my surprise I developed a fellow feeling for Blake, a genuine empathy as we would say to-day, especially when I saw how hard he drove himself to achieve results in so many different fields of human activity. And even more when I learned that, though successful, he never made much money. And still more when I learned that he did not care a fig whether or not he made money. How I sympathize. I suspect that any wife would have empathized with Mrs.Blake – Catherine Boucher – who, when asked about their family life is reported to have replied: "I see very little of Mr.Blake's company. He is always in Paradise." It was only some time after I had completed my readings of William Blake that I found he was really an Ulsterman – his father James Blake had been originally an O'Neill, a Protestant Dissenter, who moved to Golden Square, London and set up as a hosier with the name of Blake.

Like most people I live to some extent through contact and exchange with like-minded friends. Although therefore I have been stressing in this Essay the planned programme of private reading which I had set myself in my Seventies, the effort was by no means as solitary as it may sound. I have bounced my impressions off my well-read daughters-in-law, for example. And I enjoyed telling my friend Winifred Briggs – something of a specialist in English literature herself – the progress I was making. When I came to the novel and started to pick out the novelist who stood up best to the test of time, Winifred interrupted me by saying: "I can tell which novelist you are going to mention. George Eliot". And she was right. Adam Bede, despite its setting of early nineteenth century rural paternalism, could stand alongside any of the present-day novels so far as sheer quality of writing and human interest are concerned. And as for Silas Marner it remains for me the perfect novel.

If Arnold Bennett were living and writing to-day, he would almost certainly be a giant of television. His racy, light readable novels combined with his lively journalism would mark him out for a high place among the sitcoms. Just imagine Denry Machin challenging Eastenders in the ratings or Coronation Street being rivalled by an Anna of the Five Towers written specially for T.V. or his austere articles in The Academy being read on Radio. Being the versatile character he was Arnold Bennett would, I feel sure, have got his work on to all channels simultaneously.

Beaumont and Fletcher, Bishop Berkeley, Colly Cibber, Jeremy Taylor, Jeremy Bentham – especially Bentham, the Utilitarian Philosopher who propounded so many ideas at once forward-looking and practical in the real world of prison reform, the voting system, the jury system, merchant shipping, the drafting of Acts of Parliament, savings banks, friendly societies, postage, census returns, registration of births, deaths and marriages – where did they all come from? What sort of lives did they lead? What spurred them on to write? I really don't know. I suppose I must now make another fresh start, drop everything else, and fill in these gaps in my knowledge. And after that . . .

On the Stormont Administration 1921–72

The Difficult Beginnings

Before trying to describe, much less assess, the Administration under the Government of Northern Ireland it is important to recall the circumstances in which it began.

Neither self-government nor any form of devolved government had been sought. The unionist majority in the North of Ireland had opposed Home Rule in any shape; their demand had simply been for the union with Britain.

When the settlement came in 1920 and the British Parliament passed the Government of Ireland Act of that year, the people of Northern Ireland found that devolved government had been given to them as part of a wider scheme for devolved government in the South as well, a Council of all Ireland and eventually a united Ireland. Once it became clear that these three latter provisions were not likely to come about under the Act, the unionist majority in the North found themselves saddled with some truncated fragments of a complex but largely redundant statute. Constitutional instability was therefore statutorily built into the new system from the start.

In more practical terms, no plans had been made – no Provisional Government, no blueprint, no chief officials ear-marked and quietly making preparations. What is more, Belfast had never been a capital city and therefore had none of the apparatus or institutions of government High Court, stationery office, registry of deeds, public record office or corps of experienced parliamentary and departmental officers, to say nothing of suitable premises. Much worse, Ireland was in a state of civil war between opposing forces within the Nationalist community in Ireland. There was turmoil everywhere, uncertainty about the intentions of the British government, doubt even about responsibility for military and police services.[1] And yet the Administration was quickly set up and the new Parliament opened on 7 June 1921. The first Parliamentary Question was put on 20 September and the first numbered Question printed on the Order Paper on 26 September 1921, dealing with arms allegedly brought in by Sinn Fein.

The essential offices of the Audit, the Exchequer and of the Consolidated Fund were established, all under a Comptroller and Auditor General. A series of departments came into being: Finance, Labour, Home Affairs, Education and Commerce with Agriculture (later to be separated). A Parliamentary Draftsman of some considerable distinction started on the long, intricate path of preparing the Bills for Parliament. The Ministry of Finance rapidly established its authority over the spending departments. Each departmental head – the Permanent Secretary became the Accounting Officer directly responsible for all income and expenditure including the placing of contracts (a vital step that did much to establish the clear, impartial control so essential to good government).

The Administration was headed by experienced civil servants either transferred or borrowed from Dublin, London or Edinburgh. They naturally adopted the four British principles of anonymity and confidentiality (later relaxed a little at the edges as social conditions changed) and impartiality and incorruptibility (firmly maintained to the present day). The Dubliners in particular brought wit, culture, grace and charm and left a strong imprint on our Administration.

Given the small size of the Administration it was easy to avoid some of the stuffiness and rigidity of the much larger British system; officers knew one another personally; Christian names were commonly used; and of course the prevailing Irish atmosphere of informality helped as well. In general we adopted the well-tried structure of a spine, so to speak, of all-purpose, non-specialist administrators flanked by professional, technical and specialist advisers. The alternative system was that followed in the Ministries of Agriculture and Education where specialists took over administrative positions, often indeed the top positions. And there were many individual cases in other departments of professional and technical officers taking on administrative responsibilities. It was hard to draw any conclusions about the relative merits; both systems were made to work.[2]

Indeed 'made to work' was the watchword of a great deal of the Administration. It is ironic, but undoubtedly significant, that a Province that did not seek or want devolution should have been so outstandingly successful in making it work. Two examples confirm that assertion. The many functions of government were classified in the 1920 Act as transferred, reserved and excepted. There lay a most fruitful field for bureaucratic friction and legalistic conflict with London over definition, responsibility, border-lines, overlap, precedent, decided Court cases and so on. But although there was plenty of argument and occasional disagreement there was little or no conflict. That abstruse classification of functions was made to work from 1921 till 1972.[3] Similarly the financial system was not such an arcane mystery as some make out but firmly handled by a few dedicated experts in the Ministry of Finance and the British Treasury with the Ministry of Finance keeping a clear eye on what really mattered to them, namely the Residuary Share of Reserved Taxation (that part of Westminster revenue raised in Northern Ireland which was made available to us).

The three broad bands of staffing and activity in the Administration were maintained – clerical, executive and administrative – but without rigidity and with plenty of upward movement for successful and promising staff under flexible arrangements. 'Every clerk carries a Permanent Secretary's carpet in his brief-case' was the informal slogan and in fact some of the ablest Heads did rise from the lowliest beginnings, a healthy feature of our system. We may even have invented one small tool of good, informal, integrated administration – the Monday Morning Meeting- a firm arrangement adopted in many of our offices under which groups of senior officers met for an hour (without an agenda and without any minutes) simply to talk over their problems, let off steam, ask questions, seek help or put out warnings of storms brewing. In that way no senior man was in a position to say 'I never knew' or 'Nobody ever tells me anything' or 'I haven't even seen my boss for ages'.[4] This was of course in addition to all normal business meetings.

Four Phases

Those of us who lived through it all, or through most of it, saw the Administration in about four phases. First, 1921–39 when the problems were of getting a system of government going, of trying to establish law and order, of facing heavy unemployment in years of world-wide depression and of laying the foundations for the whole structure of cash benefits which was to carry (with such exemplary efficiency and economy) such a heavy load as social and economic policies gradually changed. Before we move on to the second phase – the war years – it may be helpful to have an academic, impartial and thoroughly researched assessment of the Administration in 1939: Professor J. W. Blake in his official history of the war:

The architects of Government in Northern Ireland, by a combination of skill, determination, hard work and imagination, had by 1939 produced a working system of administration capable of adaption without undue loss of efficiency in the event of an emergency. The machinery of government, central and local, was in fact at once made available on the outbreak of war. If not perfect it had stood the test of nearly twenty years of hard experience. The circumstances of the genesis of Northern Ireland, being unusual, had called for much improvisation on the part of the civil service and the staff of the local authorities. The lessons learned in such a school were likely to prove useful in time of war when flexibility and improvisation often become imperative. Among the assets which Northern Ireland could boast, the men and women employed in the service of government should justly be given a prominent place (Chapter 1).[5]

The war years proved difficult but satisfying. Where Britain had flinched at the prospect of imposing conscription on Ulster in the face of likely armed resistance we had the task of running the wartime services in face of similar difficulties: some of the population in varying degrees out of sympathy with the war effort; and a neutral country on our land border. A. R. P. street wardens, black-out measures, casualty services, rescue services, fire services and, most difficult of all, evacuation arrangements just had to be organised both before and throughout heavy German bombing raids on Belfast with 850 of our people killed (the statistical equivalent of some 35,000 in Great Britain); and all on top of the whole business of manufacturing munitions and helping to feed the British population.

It is right to record that, in the event, and in spite of British fears, many of our Catholic friends, colleagues and others supported the war, some with great distinction, including a Victoria Cross winner.

1945 to 1968 were without a doubt the golden years, the years of confidence and of positive achievement in all departments, years in which we were able to show that good administration could be made to work in spite of political division in the community and in spite of periodic IRA violence.

But of course turmoil came back in 1968; violence erupted, hasty changes had to be made; and we learned the sad lesson that violence does pay. Continuing violence on the streets turned out to be the main factor moving the British Government to suspend the Administration in March 1972 and bring in Direct Rule.

In Letters of Gold

At the obvious cost of being selective and possibly unfair to colleagues, let us pick out some of the outstanding achievements of the Administration. First, making the system work as a whole despite a badly fragmented written constitution, attacks on the constitution from outside and inside, Articles 2 and 3 of the Eire Constitution, a derisory amount of independent revenue and the limited authority and standing of a small devolved government.

Second, a fine record in the preparation and simplification of Parliamentary legislation and in the supervision of the difficult and controversial field of subordinate legislation made by departments (statutory rules and orders) that so directly affect the citizen in his home or his work. Our innovative Interpretation Act reduced the volume of the statutes by as much as one third and was widely followed in the English speaking world. In spite of all our difficulties we managed to play a modest part on the world stage, refusing to become provincial.

Third, the assessment and prompt payment of cash benefits to a large section of the population under laws and principles that over the 51 years changed many times with changing conditions. The practical task of running the benefit offices under conditions of violence and the threat of violence needs to be experienced to be understood. At times of special difficulty our benefit staffs even had to fight their way through street disorders in order to reach their offices and pay out benefits to the very people who were creating these disorders.

In any divided society one of the acid tests is how the Administration treats the minority in the matter of schooling. After battling to set up a County system in the 1920s; after succeeding with the greatest difficulty in persuading the Protestant Churches to transfer their schools to it (a bitter struggle): after then finding that the Roman Catholic Church declined totally and irrevocably to hand over their schools: a Ministry of Education might have abandoned the Catholic schools to their fate and given them scant help or consideration. Instead, the Stormont Administration went out of its way to face the facts realistically, to study what was being done in Scotland, to acknowledge and then to promote a fully fledged voluntary sector within the education system at the levels of primary and secondary schooling and of teacher training (but not of course at University level which throughout remained wholly integrated and nondenominational). Financial support was good and, after 1945, generous in the extreme. Relations concerning curriculum, inspection, examinations and management were handled with tact and understanding on both sides. All this is fully understood and confirmed by the Catholic school authorities, but seldom recognised publicly by their political spokesmen. One outcome has of course been a system of Catholic schools across the Province of the highest quality.[6]

Another educational achievement by the Administration was the settlement in 1947 of the universal secondary school system, free of charge and embodying the principle of selection for grammar, intermediate and technical schools according to ability, aptitude and parental choice. Within the grammar school system a non-denominational County sector ran alongside a stronger voluntary sector (Catholic, Protestant and non-denominational) that was, in turn, distinguished by even finer degrees of independence both administrative and financial – the A Schools and the B Schools – based on a simple type of voucher system and permitting the charging of a small additional fee for capital purposes strictly controlled by law (and, at £3 originally, willingly paid by parents). These grammar schools are today amongst the finest in the United Kingdom, with sixth-form leavers being not only accepted but actively sought out by Admissions Tutors from Oxford and Cambridge. Despite many attacks this system has survived for over 40 years and whatever may be said by its critics it is phenomenally popular with parents.

We were not a bit surprised in any way to find that the many innovations and new departures forged here after much political and administrative struggle evoked little interest in England. (There was more understanding in Scotland of what we were achieving on our own.) One exception was in the field of agriculture research and teaching; that did create interest in relevant circles in England, and at first raised some eyebrows amongst purists on grounds of possible loss of academic freedom, but eventually came to be recognised as an imaginative and successful scheme .

What happened was this. The Ministry of Agriculture, the most uninhibited of all our departments, made sure from the earliest years that research, teaching, farm advice and administration would be forged into one coherent unit. They helped to set up the Faculty of Agriculture at The Queen's University of Belfast, arranging that its Professors, Heads of Departments and other lecturers became also, at the same time, advisers in the Ministry – Plant Pathology, Animal Husbandry, Field Botany, Entomology, Biometrics, and so on. In that way the Ministry had immediately available to it the very top advice; the Professors far from being in an ivory tower had the sobering benefit of practical experience gleaned from the farms.

All of that knowledge was then easily conveyed to the Ministry's inspectors and advisers out in the field and brought to bear on work on the farms. More than that, the Ministry (instead of leaving agricultural schools and colleges to the local education authorities) ran them – Greenmount, Loughry, Enniskillen and so on – from the Ministry under what we used to call 'direct drive', again enjoying the great benefit of top level scientific advice from men who were all colleagues in the same team. It must be said that this independent and unique system became deeply rooted and immensely popular in the whole agricultural fraternity. More important, it proved effective in raising standards in matters such as animal health (including tuberculosis, brucellosis, Johne's disease, foot and mouth), immune potato seed and a great deal else. Food Science was then added to the scope of the Ministry and the Faculty.

A severe test arose in the 1960s when the New University of Ulster was being planned and when, with its bias toward biology and ecology, it had a strong claim to take over the Faculty of Agriculture and move the research establishments to Coleraine. There followed one of the sharpest arguments any of us could recall but the success of the Stormont experiment and its popularity won the day.

This may be a convenient point at which to record the early and energetic spread of electricity, carrying power and light to every townland. In addition to all its other benefits, electricity (together with Harry Ferguson's invention of the tractor and its successors) revolutionised life even on our smallest farms.

One of the most immediately apparent features of present-day Ulster is the splendid road system. Here we had a textbook example of political and administrative collaboration in pursuit of a clear goal. Ministers were determined after 1945 to have the most up-to-date road system throughout the Province, partly for the convenience and safety of their citizens and partly in order to encourage new industry and tourism. Their argument was that as industrialists and tourists had to be enticed to cross the sea to reach Ulster, they ought not then to find themselves bogged down in country roads but should be able to reach all parts within an hour or so from the main International Airport. Ministers therefore gave every encouragement to Departments to get on with that job. The outcome was a streamlined unit for the planning, design, construction and management of roads and bridges that became the envy of road-builders throughout the Kingdom. To those of us in the Administration it was no accident and no surprise that some of the finest and earliest roads and bridges were built in County Londonderry. The clear wish of Ministers to see good roads and bridges serving Londonderry as soon as possible coincided, by one of those happy chances of history, with the activities of a particularly lively and positive County Surveyor (Harold Scott) who knew how to work the system for the benefit of his county and to outpace some of his colleagues in other areas.

One innovation in the field of Road Safety was the setting up of a Vehicle Inspectorate, a body charged with the duty of carrying out tests for roadworthiness; this system differs from that introduced in Great Britain where commercial garages are authorised to carry them out. Another step which might usefully be copied in Great Britain today was the 'R' plate for newly qualified drivers, restricting them to 45 miles an hour in those heady months after they pass their driving test.

It is important always to remember that violence and security do occupy an inordinate amount of time and resources. It is all too often forgotten (when asking the rhetorical questions: why did the Administration not do more about this or that?) that the IRA kept up a sustained campaign of violence, bombing, shooting and murder (mainly in rural areas) for six years from 1956 till 1962 (as well as always casting a threatening shadow from 1921 on. By unremitting effort the Royal Ulster Constabulary and the B Specials kept that campaign under control until the IRA, failing to win any support from outside Ulster, saw there was no future in it and gave up. Before dismissing the B Specials as merely a sectarian paramilitary force, one would be wise to read the account of 'B Men', written by Wallace Clark in 1971.[7]

One of the many original steps, and one of the most successful, taken by the Administration independently of Britain in order to deal with a special problem, was the setting up of the Northern Ireland Tuberculosis Authority in 1946. Tuberculosis, for long under British rule a terrible scourge in Ireland, had been exposed during the War as the third killing disease in the population and the first killing disease amongst young adults. The idea was to create a small body specially equipped to focus all the preventive and remedial measures and dedicated to the eradication of the disease, independent of the main new Health Service then being set up. In ten years or so NITA was able to declare itself redundant, its job done. Scottish administrators were envious.

In the important field of personal social services that touch so closely on individual and family life we advanced in two big steps independently of Great Britain. First, when we were re-shaping health and welfare after the war we went out of our way to legislate specially for a distinctive welfare service, independent of medical administration and not subordinate to the Doctors as the medical profession would have wished at that time. Our law obliged each County and County Borough Council in 1949 to set up a statutory Welfare Committee and to appoint not only a statutory Welfare Officer but also a statutory Welfare Secretary. That law was unique in the United Kingdom and it served to bring about a confident welfare service with its own standards and ethos in every corner of Ulster.

When, then, those services had had time to prove themselves, to build up their professional standing, training and qualifications and to throw up further problems in social care, we were able by 1971 to move on and merge them with the health services under the four Health and Social Services Boards then being planned. The result was the integrated arrangement which we have today in every corner of the land, with social welfare standing on a dignified footing comparable with medicine, nursing, pharmacy, dentistry and so on – four-square in the main stream of health and welfare provision, influencing the other parts and being influenced by them.

In that way we closed the gap (so glaringly obvious in Great Britain) between the National Health Service and the local authority social service, and (perhaps more important) we closed the absurd gulf between funding out of taxation and funding out of rating in, for example, the care of the elderly, the handicapped and the mentally ill. When we look today at the terrible problems of child abuse in England and the difficulty experienced there in bringing medical and social care into harness for the sake of those tormented children we may be pardoned for thinking that perhaps we did not do too badly for ours.

Meanwhile, as is well known and in a much bigger framework, our Health Service was going from strength to strength. Under the Northern Ireland Hospitals Authority many fine new hospitals and hospital extensions were built in the 1950s and 1960s – in Londonderry, Enniskillen, Omagh, Dungannon, Magherafelt, Gransha near Londonderry, for example, in step with, and often before, comparable improvements in the East of the Province. Any suggestion that we favoured Belfast and the East over the West of the Province would get an extremely cool reception at the Belfast Hospital for Sick Children, the Royal Maternity Hospital and the Belfast City (former Poor Law) Hospital- all key hospitals that were forced to work in old unsuitable buildings while watching glittering buildings go up elsewhere.

Then the full marriage of hospital, general practice, community medicine, social welfare and related scientific services could take place in the 1970s, giving an up-to-date, humane and flexible service to our people; not just up-to-date but, in relation to some aspects of surgery in a situation of constant terrorism, ahead of the world.[8]

Much nonsense is talked about the failure or the refusal or the neglect of the Administration to locate new or expanded industries west of the River Bann. An enormous amount of thought and effort was devoted by the Ministry of Commerce to that very problem. But they had no powers of direction. Their task was to invite industrialists, encourage them, offer them grants (including substantially higher grants for factories in the more remote areas) loans, subsidies or other inducements and do all they could to persuade them to settle in the remoter towns and villages. As the years went on they succeeded to a surprising degree: Du Pont and British Oxygen at Maydown

Londonderry, Daintyfit in Limavady, Hoechst near Limavady, Chemstrand at Coleraine, Adria at Strabane, Taylor Woods and English Sewing Cotton in Fermanagh and many others. These were concrete achievements.

In the earlier years the bigger industrialists had been harder to persuade to go to far-flung places at a time when roads, bridges, culverts, water supplies and much else were still only being developed. This was perfectly understandable in many cases. Even in the later years industrialists naturally had their own ideas and their own priorities. Distance and transport were obviously dominant. Supply of labour, sometimes of skilled engineering labour, was another. But there were many other requirements of a deeper nature. A pure water supply was important to many and takes time to organise, as was brilliantly done by an inventive scheme on the River Faughan at Maydown, for example, in support of Du Pont from Delaware. Disposal of noxious effluent was a particularly intractable problem as was discovered at Chemstrand – and solved. Ordinary sewerage provision takes time – more time than water supply- and in small communities can present surprising difficulties. Housing for workers, housing for executives, technical education, industrial training – all these can easily be demanded in the location of industry, to say nothing of improvement to roads, bridges and culverts to take heavy industrial traffic where none ever flowed previously.

Thousands of man-hours, high-level outside professional advice, massive inter-departmental study and a lot of travel were devoted to the problems of promoting industry in Fermanagh, Tyrone, Londonderry and Armagh. Even if the Ministry of Commerce had lagged in those efforts – which they certainly did not – they would have been spurred on by the Ministry of Development whose policies involved restricting the growth of Belfast (for many sound reasons), building up growth centres and lesser growth towns in every part of the Province as part of their sophisticated and ambitious ideas of integrated urban development within an unspoiled green countryside and a pattern of amenity lands and areas of special scientific interest. As an example of co-ordinated industrial and civic development backed by a flexible programme of infrastructure within a regional plan those efforts stood up well to comparison with similar endeavours in other parts of the United Kingdom.[9]

On a different note entirely it is right to add here that throughout all those vigorous programmes, man-to-man contacts with forceful industrialists and huge outlay of public money we had no scandals in the Administration, no cases of bribery in the departments and a less than normal quota of minor defalcations and frauds. Taking all in all, then, it is little wonder that Professor W. N. Osborough should see fit to write in *The Irish Jurist*, Volume XII, pages 389-92: 'Were it not for the inherent instability in the order of things and the violence and civil strife that took over in the years after 1968, the achievements of Northern Ireland Civil Service might well have been written in letters of gold.'

Criticism, Complaints, Grievances

Any Administration working under a parliamentary and democratic system is open to constant criticism as part of the healthy process; and the Stormont Administration got its fair share from every quarter. Our many day-to-day shortcomings would have been hard to conceal in a small community where 'everyone knew everyone'. In a sense the very smallness of the administrative area (as well as the blunt tone of public comment in Ulster) lent itself to outspoken criticism of departments. And we contributed further to our problems by our open-door policy of readiness to receive Deputations at the drop of a hat: 'You people receive more Deputations from the six counties in a month than we in Dublin used to do in a year from the whole of Ireland'.[10]

The Royal Commission on the (British) Constitution[11] dealt tellingly and amusingly with this feature of Stormont Administration:

Even the most severe critic of home rule amongst our witnesses . . . considered the devolution of administrative and executive powers to have been an outstanding success. He argued . . . a dissatisfied farmer anywhere within its boundaries ought to be able (and is able) to travel by public transport to the administrative capital, horse-whip the responsible official and get home again (in time to milk the cow).

For those of us at the receiving end horse-whipping is painful and is relieved only slightly by the knowledge that one of the motives was to be able to tell the neighbours back home how well he had dealt with 'those boys up at Stormont'. Perhaps even the very fact of the main Administrative Building being sited on a prominent hill outside the City of Belfast made it an easier object for criticism. The farmer and his cow are reminders of the deeply rural and agricultural background of many Ulster people. To them the sight of well-paid and pensionable officials in comfortable offices understandably sharpened the edge of their criticism.

But there were of course deeper and more deeply-felt criticisms. In the eyes of the nationalist population from the very start Stormont had a pervasive aura of unionism. This arose to some extent from the policy of giving preference in employment to ex-servicemen (many of whom had lost an eye or a limb in the First World War) and of maintaining the King's National Roll (giving preference in jobs to ex-servicemen). Despite the fact that both were entirely honourable and fully in tune with public opinion and despite the fact that beneficiaries were largely employed in lowly jobs (and poorly paid), there is little doubt that as doorkeepers, messengers and counter-clerks they gave the impression of unionist and loyalist hirelings in the early years of the Administration.

Much more important were the grievances published at home and abroad by the nationalist population in connection with employment, housing, location of industry, electoral affairs, the Royal Ulster Constabulary, the B Specials, the Courts of Law Special Powers and much else of which we in the Administration were of course well aware. It was no pleasure to us as ordinary sensitive family men and householders to hear complaints about unfairness and disadvantage. Besides, to the extent that any of the complaints turned out to be justified, that would have reflected on our conduct of various services. And of course complaints always mean more work, more briefing of Ministers, more drafting of letters and so on – all of which distracts from the more creative work which we were so keen to push on with.

Attendance in the officials' pew of the Commons or Senate was for the most part a depressing chore, for we had to listen to an endless recital of complaints, right or wrong, justified or unjustified, repetitive, whinging and wholly negative in approach. Every Government move was opposed,[12] every Minister denounced, every grievance magnified. We often used to wish we could have been permitted to brief the Opposition and provide draft speeches, for we knew we could have given them much more promising and constructive lines of approach, hitting the Government at points where we knew they were truly vulnerable.[13]

Acts of Parliament and administrative memoranda, no matter how splendid, matter little to the man in the street. What matters to him is how the Administration affects him at the sharp end. This is where many of our difficulties arose and where many of the grievances were nourished. The further you got from the headquarters of the departments the closer you got to the political battlefield, to the cockpit of unionist versus nationalist, of house tenancies, of job allocation, of voting and of political violence.

Let us take housing as an example both of an important service and of a fruitful ground for complaint. Of the scores of Housing Acts passed at Stormont, none was ever challenged in the Courts. (Very few of all the hundreds of statutes passed were ever challenged in the High Court on constitutional grounds and even then only on a technicality not affecting civil rights in any way. We thought this significant in itself and took comfort from it at the time.)

Criticism centred on the location of Council housing estates in relation to electoral wards and on the subsequent allocation of tenancies; a mountain of propaganda has been built on that matter. One is in honour bound to record that many local authorities acted blamelessly in those matters – for example Bangor, North Down, Holywood, Antrim Rural, Ballymoney Urban, Coleraine Borough. Most others, beset by political problems struggled manfully to maintain standards and do the right thing. This applies with particular force to the Belfast Corporation (our biggest local authority by far) which, despite serious problems on the Falls Road for generations, kept up a fine standard of fairness in housing matters – and for which it has gained little credit.

This leaves only a small minority of councils in the areas of more or less equal and uneasy balance in their communities, in the outlying border areas who took up the defensive position and are therefore accused of using their housing powers to protect their electoral majorities; but as they saw the position, they were trying to protect the Province and to protect the frontiers of the United Kingdom across its one and only land border. If their methods were wrong and unwise, their motives and their circumstances have to be understood.

Councils controlled by nationalists were of course playing similar games though we always warned that that provided no excuse.[14] For most of the 1921–72 period 11 out of the 67 local councils under criticism were nationalist or even outright republican and when faced with reality were, like the unionist councils, in a most difficult position. Was a scarce tenancy to be given to some reliable unionist, perhaps a member of the Royal Ulster Constabulary, who could be counted on to pay his rent and to keep his house and garden in good condition? Or was it to be given to a 'feckless' nationalist, who might not pay his rent regularly nor keep the property well, who was a constant critic of the state, who flew the Eire Tricolor flag on his dwelling, carried a Dublin passport and put an Eire plate on the back of his car? That, bluntly, was how the council often saw the issue of a tenancy in those tense situations.

In the welter of accusations against local housing authorities from 1968 until 1972, the work of the Northern Ireland Housing Trust was barely mentioned – another of our Ulster initiatives – a body unique in the British Isles with distinguished achievements in planning,, locating, designing and managing attractive estates (held in widespread esteem) and with an impeccable record of fair, unbiased allocation regardless of electoral considerations.

We must be especially outspoken on this matter. If discrimination in housing had been in the mind of the Administration and one of its purposes – even in the most passive and secretive sense – then to set up the Housing Trust immediately after the War was a funny way of going about it. Here we deliberately created a statutory authority alongside the local councils, manned by prominent people of strongly independent mind (some highly critical of the Unionist Government), well funded, well staffed and playing an active role in housing deliberations in the United Kingdom (and highly regarded there). Far from holding the Trust back in any sense the Administration's aim was to push the Trust on to build ever more houses at the cost of incurring a heavier burden of debt which the Quakerly gentlemen at the head of the Trust always seemed to us to be reluctant to do. And what about our unique Private Enterprise Subsidy Scheme, administered by the Ministry with no powers of decision resting with the local councils, immensely popular throughout the whole Province? Did no nationalists benefit- either under the Owner Occupation section or the Building for Lettings section? And what about tenancies under independent voluntary Housing Associations? And what about our quiet but highly effective Housing on Farms scheme, again either for occupation or for letting – deliberately run on a confidential basis by the Ministry itself (but resulting, we fear, in some extremely ugly dwellings of crude suburban design in beautiful farming land)? And what about our self-help (or Self-Build as we inelegantly called it) scheme enabling really enterprising fellows actually to erect their own houses with their own hands?

We kept no tally of the religion of occupiers, of course, but it would have come as no surprise to anyone in the Administration to find in 1972 that there were as many Catholics in subsidised modern housing as Protestants, indeed, possibly more, if children were added in. The big housing estates built by the Belfast Corporation (Divis Flats, Turf Lodge and Ballymurphy) along with Andersontown, the Creggan, estates built by the 11 nationalist councils, the 40,000 tenancies allocated by the Housing Trust and the remaining local authorities, the private enterprise government schemes of all kinds – all would have provided testimony in any such count on top of the figures in the 1971 Census Returns.

But, going even more deeply into the subject, no-one is obliged to look all the time to the state (in its various manifestations) for housing. More than half of our stock of dwelling houses remained in private ownership – individual or commercial.[15]

Even in the field of local council electoral boundaries – the one field of complaint with some basis of fact and the one that was badly handled by the Administration – there has been enormous distortion and exaggeration. The emotive cry 'One Man One Vote' which evoked such sympathy all around the world was contrived to convey a story of total denial of democracy whereas the factual position was very different. For one thing, universal adult franchise applied to Stormont elections and to Westminster election: emphasis on the ratepayers' franchise applied only to elections for local councils and was based on the perfectly reasonable principle of 'he who pays the piper calls the tune' – a principle that held good in Great Britain until the end of the Second World War.

In the same way the undoubted inequities of some local electoral boundaries (again for local councils only, not for Stormont or for Westminster) were so publicised as to obscure the fact that nationalist councillors in some District Electoral Divisions were being returned on derisorily small votes.[16] Worse still, unionist areas of heavy populations around Belfast were forced by the Stormont Administration to keep out-of-date wards and to have unionist councillors returned with enormous and quite unwieldy electorates as a deliberate if clumsy counter-balance to nationalist under-representation in some areas, pending a complete overhaul of local government in due course.[17] It was a tragedy that the whole local government system which we inherited from Britain in 1921 too many councils, too small, too poor, too ill-equipped and too exposed to political tension – had not been overhauled in the years 1945–48 when so much else was being turned upside down. That would have been the time to do it.[18]

On the main subject, again, of nationalist complaints against the Administration we who thought that there were few of any importance could well have been wrong. For all we knew we could have been burying our busy heads in the sand and there could have been pent-up floods of justified complaints ready to burst upon us.

One way of finding out would be to appoint an Ombudsman. In the Departments we had been inclined to advise against any such appointment: first because it would be merely a fifth wheel on the coach of a small, efficient and responsive Administration subject already to far too many constraints; and second because we foresaw that the very existence of such an Officer would have the effect of causing civil servants to be unduly cautious over their paper-work, dotting every 'i' and crossing every 't' whereas the needs of the situation called for even greater boldness and initiative. Ministers also were against the idea on the ground that we already had 52 Ombudsmen in the Members of the Commons; that bringing forward the concerns of constituents was a side of their work which they and their constituents valued; and that an Ombudsman would undermine and devalue a representative House of Commons in such a small community.

When however the decision was made to appoint one, we went out of our way to get the best: Sir Edmund Compton who not only had the experience of being Ombudsman for the United Kingdom administration but was actually serving in that capacity. He was thus in the unique position of overseeing administration both in Northern Ireland and in the whole of the United Kingdom at one and the same time. Where was the terrible flood of complaints? There was none; nothing but a trickle of perfectly ordinary cases that revealed no corpus of maladministration whatever. The Ombudsman in his first Report went on to declare: 'it is fair to say the quality of administrative performance in the Northern Ireland Ministries compares well with my experience of Government Departments in the United Kingdom. Indeed the individual citizen frequently gets a better service from a Northern Ireland

Ministry than he would get from a United Kingdom Department . . .'.[19] And facing a Press Conference, reported in the *Belfast Telegraph* on 27 January 1971, he said he had found high quality of administration in the central (Stormont) government – almost to a fault. An individual here received noticeably higher consideration than those in any other part of the United Kingdom. From the point of view of efficiency it was almost too high; for the citizen it was all to the good. There was not one incident of culpable action by any organ of central government.[20]

Admittedly, of course, one Ombudsman could be mistaken; perhaps his successors would unearth a terrible heap of burning complaints? They did not. The Ombudsman deals only with the administration of central government not with that of local government. That might be where the real body of justified complaints would be revealed to the world. We therefore created yet another office: The Commissioner for Complaints. He too found little or nothing of substance.

However, Ombudsmen can investigate only those complaints which came before them under certain rules. They cannot roam at will over the whole field and examine such aspects as they think right. What was needed was the experience not of one man but a balanced body of several men and women of widely different backgrounds with an open remit. That would be a task for a Royal Commission. We were lucky in that Britain had in 1969 set up a prestigious Commission to examine the workings of the British Constitution both centrally and locally and with particular stress on the various parts of the kingdom. They sat for four years and took much evidence in Ulster.[21] The Royal Commission endorsed the findings of the first Ombudsman; gave the Administration a clean bill of health; and went out of its way to conclude: 'We were left in no doubt that at the time of our visit the people of Northern Ireland believed that they derived substantial advantages from administrative devolution, and we accepted that this belief was well founded.'[22] A hefty and learned Memorandum of Dissent (on other matters) running to 221 pages of close print took nothing at all away from those conclusions.

All in all those of us who served in the Administration are convinced both from our own experiences and from those totally impartial judgements that the so-called grievances and complaints that have been publicized all over the world have been hugely exaggerated. Complaint, like beauty, is in the eye of the beholder. As in human behaviour generally, those who complain are often reflecting unresolved conflicts within themselves.

We knew perfectly well that there were much more profound reasons. To begin with, that endearing Irish tendency to exaggerate, to call every hill a mountain, and every village a town, had to be guarded against when every adverse administrative decision became a case of tyranny and oppression. We knew that the deeper reasons lay in the political refusal to recognise the state and to support the actual legal and fiscal situation which all of us were in together. The political views and aspirations of individual citizens were of no concern to us; what did concern us was the way in which nationalist leaders used particular faults, mistakes or shortcomings to denigrate the state and try to pull it down. Political opposition, it must always be remembered, was aimed not just at the Party in power: it was aimed at the existence of the State; and political defence, in response, was aimed not only at defence of the Party but of the State and ultimately of the United Kingdom. That was the framework within which our administration had to be carried on and within which grievances were promoted.

On the question of poverty in the nationalist community Paul Arthur deals with the matter with great delicacy and humour in *Government and Politics of Northern Ireland*.[23] He brings out some amusing quotations which Rosemary Harris records from people she interviewed:[24]

She was sure Catholics had no scruples about trying to abuse the Health Service and indeed that they felt politically virtuous in doing so. There's not a Roman Catholic in the country, she said, that hasn't two pairs of spectacles and false teeth. Catholic doctors, she thought were always ready to say a Catholic was sick even when he was healthy if only it would get him government money.

After recording that characteristic set of views, Arthur comments dryly: 'Catholic poverty was a result of their own fecklessness and made undue demands on the welfare state'.

One aspect which distressed us greatly in the Administration was the accumulation of debt, with all its attendant human sufferings, as a direct result of the Rent and Rates Strike in nationalist areas in the late summer of 1971. This highly political strike following internment may or may not have been justified; but what was most certainly not justified was the advice given to humble tenants to spend their rent money (instead of putting it safely away behind the clock) in the mistaken belief that a soft government would one day grant an amnesty, when all would be forgiven. That cruel advice was enforced by slogans painted on the pavements in nationalist housing estates: RENT SPENT. While making every humane allowance for the unhappiness of innocent people burdened with debt and dogged by most complicated legal and administrative measures to recover the money due to the public purse for years after the event, it is impossible to see that particular complaint of poverty and social distress in nationalist areas as a ground for any possible complaint against the public authorities. Put another way, that terrible and fully authenticated experience makes it much harder to put credence in some other complaints by nationalist leaders.

Let us now turn the subject of complaints around and look at it from yet another point of view. If the saga of complaints and grievances had started only after executive government had got into its stride in 1922 and petered out after 1972, then there would have been reasonable presumption that the complaints arose out of or were actually caused by actions of the Administration 1921–72. The facts throw that presumption out of the window.

Well before any decisions were taken affecting the people, objection and obstruction had started: the new parliament was boycotted; some constituencies returned Members from the Irish Free State who could not possibly take their seats; and some local authorities persisted in sending their Minutes and Accounts to Dublin instead of Belfast.

Long after the Administration was wound up in 1972 complaints against police, prisons and courts persist. To take two up-to-date examples: in September 1988 television cameras focused carefully on an IRA wall slogan in Belfast: 'IRA the voice of an oppressed people' and television companies broadcast it around the world.

Much more insidious is the situation revealed by a letter from the first Director of Public Prosecutions, Sir Barry Shaw, published in *The Guardian* on Saturday, 10 September 1988:

The article (September 5) by David Pallister and Richard Norton-Taylor contained the allegation that in the cases investigated by Mr Stalker it had emerged that RUC officers had, on one occasion, lied under oath on instructions from the Director of Public Prosecutions' office in Belfast.

I write to inform you and place on record that this allegation is untrue and without any foundation in fact whatsoever.

(Sir) Barry Shaw
The Royal Courts of Justice,
Belfast

That terse, firm letter is significant on three levels. First, it confirms that false and unfounded complaints against the established public authorities are still being made after 19 years of impartial British rule. Second, it also confirms that investigators and the English Press are still grazing on garbage and being taken in by blarney. Third, and perhaps most seriously, it suggests that a whole fresh cycle of complaint is now developing, complaint against new public institutions demanded in order to deal with complaints and granted in order to appease the critics. The Police Authority is another. No doubt the Fair Employment Agency will be pulled down in its turn; and, who knows, the Ombudsman, the Commissioner for Complaints, and so on and so on.

Much political and sociological literature in recent years has spoken not of individual complaints or practical grievances but of the 'felt situation', of 'perceived grievances', 'the sense not of personal but of community loss', and so on. This article has not tried to follow those obscure paths but to concentrate on issues that ordinary people like the present writer can grasp and size up for themselves.

Of the many Public Inquiries into our affairs held over the years the one which touched most closely on the controversial and hotly disputed matters of political violence and public administration was the Inquiry into 'Disturbances in Northern Ireland' held by the Cameron Commission. This was set up in March 1969 and finished its work in August of that year, reporting in Command Paper 532 in September.

While it was valuable to have a quick and early investigation into the facts of those disturbances – what happened, who took part and why – it seemed to be too much to expect the Commission to go on and formulate mature conclusions and political recommendations in the heat of the battle, since some of the worst disturbances were actually taking place in August 1969 a mile or two away from their meeting place. The fact that there were so many witnesses – forty organisations and a couple of hundred individuals – the fact that they were not put on oath and the fact that the Commission were determined to complete their deliberations in the five months between April and August 1969 must surely have left them open to receive some, shall we say, questionable material. In that sense there is perhaps more to be learned from the detailed text of their Report than from their Summary of Conclusions (from which most public comment naturally derived).

It was a great disappointment for us to find that, although they set out clearly the large numbers of houses built by the Housing Trust, they made no analysis of the effect of the Trust's punctilious system of allocation on the overall position or as a counterbalance to that of the few small councils which they did examine. Nor did they find time to analyse and appraise the allocation of houses by our largest local council by far, the Belfast Corporation, even though they did record a number of street incidents that took place in Belfast. The fact is that the Belfast Corporation, despite terrible problems in West Belfast for a century and more, had an extremely good record of political fairness in housing matters, it must be said.

As well as all that, the Cameron Commission in 1969 were scarcely in a position to assess the revolutionary and republican influences in the early Civil Rights movement. The facts at that time were obscure and highly debatable; and events in 1969 were moving fast. If they could have read for example the commemorative issue of the Ulster journal *Fortnight* (Number 266, October 1988) and the passage about active, strong, carefully controlled participation by republicans in the Civil Rights Association written by Gerry Adams MP in *Twenty Years On* (Brandon Press, 1988), they might have been less confident in their conclusions.

Employment in the Civil Service

When the Service was being formed in 1921 many senior catholic officers chose of their own accord to transfer from Dublin and helped to form the nucleus. Some rose quickly to responsible positions.[25] A few (but not many) catholic boys then entered by the much discussed written examination system run under strict Civil Service Commission rules year by year; but they were not encouraged by their advisers to do so as Paddy Shea frankly tells in his Memoirs: *Voices and the Sound of Drums*.[26] The prevailing hostility to the new regime and the conviction that it would not last created a climate of opinion in catholic schools and families that actively discouraged entry. The outcome was as obvious as it was inevitable: with few Catholic recruits in the 1920s and 1930s, there could be few rising to the highest ranks in the 1940s, 1950s and 1960s. After the war and after seeing that the Administration had come to stay, Catholic boys and girls did start to enter; they did well; and they occupied many senior appointments.[27]

All this time direct recruitment to prominent senior professional and technical posts was going on apace; and under our well-known open-door policy many recruits came from England or Scotland. They were accepted regardless of religion or politics. The natural preponderance of Protestants coming from England and Scotland served inevitably to swell the proportions of Protestants in the Administration and to increase their prominence. A few were Catholics, of course, and the inner point here is that any hope some of us might have nourished that their presence would in some way make life easier or make the Administration more acceptable in nationalist quarters was quickly dashed. It did not make a fig of difference. (Nor incidentally did the British practice of including one Catholic Minister in each Direct Rule team after 1972 make the slightest impact on the subject of political acceptance. Religion, as we very well knew, did not matter; we were all agents of the system and as such suspect in the eyes of the opponents of the system.)

To retrace our steps a little: in 1929 the Administration took the significant step of deciding to accept year by year one or two administrative cadets (or Assistant Principals) from the famous severe and prestigious First Division Examination Competition in London. That really was a surprisingly liberal step to take, and a hostage to fortune, as there was no knowing what sort of men these were likely to be, what their religion was, what their political stance might turn out to be. Just think of Cambridge in the Thirties. In line with the reality of the times all came from Oxford and Cambridge. And of course they were likely to reach influential position in double-quick time – as in fact did Harry Jones, Hugh Lowry, David Holden and others. Did that deliberate and open policy in a key area suggest discrimination? It was not until 1937 that the first local man and graduate of the Queen's University of Belfast entered by that gate.[28] Worse still, it was not until the mid-1960s that the first Ulster Catholic graduate chose to come in by that golden gate.[29] Who was discriminating against whom all those years? The one sensitive area for the posting of Catholic civil servants had of course always been the private offices of the Ministers (each embracing one, two or three officers), including the office of the Prime Minister. Ministers had fundamentalist ideas about Catholics being subject to outside pressures and therefore not 'sound'; and they were embarrassed at the thought of a catholic private secretary ushering in a Deputation of Orangemen and taking the record of some acrimonious discussion. They need not have worried, for the officers we would have chosen to send forward would have been mature enough to acquit themselves diplomatically and indeed to see the inherent humour of the situation. But the boot was not always on the one foot, not by any means. Some Catholic officers understood the embarrassment perfectly well and, for a variety of reasons, tactfully steered clear of any such appointment. That was an open secret.

From time to time we were shown statistics drawn up by learned academics purporting to show terrible discrimination: only so many Catholics in certain ranks; only such and such a proportion when there ought to have been such and such. Hardly ever did these statistics strike us as being at all accurate or as telling the real story.

Needless to say there was disgruntlement from time to time in a disciplined service with clearly marked ranks and scales of pay. Promotion mattered; and was governed by elaborate and evolving rules painstakingly negotiated with the staff associations over the years. It was a commonplace occurrence to find that the disappointed officers who moaned most were the weaker brethren; the stronger, the more balanced, men took their inevitable disappointments a lot more stoically and could hardly be persuaded even to voice them. In all of this grumbling about promotion it is hard to recall religion playing any part whatever at the time – even amongst the weaker brethren I have mentioned. One heard instead of some other imagined cause for their failure. A common one was golf: your chances at interview and selection were so much better if you were a member of the same golf club as the Assistant Secretary or whatever. There was even a belief that if you had been to Inst you stood a much better chance than if you had simply been to Methody or Academy. It is amusing to find John Whyte recounting similar excuses used in other quarters in Belfast: preferment for lecturers at Queen's depended on having an Oxford or Cambridge degree, it seemed; and as for young surgeons at the Royal Victoria Hospital it was best to have gone to a really good rugger school.[30]

One of the fields in which the Administration failed lamentably from 1921 to 1972 was in bringing on women officers and seeing them reach the top positions. There were many admirable women in junior and middle ranks, to whom the Administration owed a great deal, but far too few at the top; indeed none. It is hard to see any convincing reason but (as with the problems affecting religious background) there may just possibly have been two sides to the story, with women seldom seeking higher responsibility (and the long hours, stress and worry that go with it in the Civil Service). Besides, of course, the full value of women in public life was not fully appreciated anywhere in those days.

One of the social policies built in to the personnel work of the Administration from the outset was the bar on the employment of married women in the Civil Service. This was very much in line with public opinion but was stubbornly maintained long after public opinion had begun to relax on the issue in the 1950s. Few Catholic married women were concerned; their family patterns and their general culture did not at that time encourage much interest. Protestant married women on the other hand were greatly interested, were clamouring at the doors and flocked in (and stayed in) as soon as the bar was eventually lifted. Here we can see a clear, proven and prolonged example of what amounted to discrimination against a Protestant group though they did not carry any grievance on that score.

Let us turn the allegations about discrimination still further on their head in order to prove how subtle and complex these matters are in actual practice at the coal-face. Many, a great many, of our former colleagues would disparage the present writer for devoting so much time and attention to allegations about discrimination. They saw themselves as managers responsible for discharging functions and for showing results. Engaged in building a telephone exchange for the British Post Office or beefing up an office to pay out sickness benefit during an epidemic, and under great pressure to meet a deadline or keep within a budget, their main concern was to get the best staff. There was intense competition for the best staff and managers cared not a fig for their religion or political background. Catholics, Protestants, Quakers, Jews– all were working side by side – with perhaps some of the Plymouth Brethren less easy colleagues than any of the others or, more likely, the rest of us (smokers and drinkers) less easy colleagues for them. That small comment is made here in order to try to convey something of the real flavour of daily life in the Administration; relations between Catholic and Protestant colleagues were easy. Those managers were beset rather by the ordinary, human problems of personality and character under office discipline. Those former colleagues would realistically dismiss the turgid heap of allegations about religious discrimination as a lot of trash.

There was talk in the late 1960s of introducing a quota system for ensuring some desired proportion of Catholics in the various ranks of the civil service. We advised strongly against, arguing that (under no matter what disguise, pretence or circumlocution) quotas lead to inefficiency, to resentment, to dissension, to loss of morale and to loss of standing in the outside world; and we knew that our Catholic colleagues were against the idea, too, as they had no wish to be stigmatised as 'quota men' or 'there only to make up a percentage'. We argued that merit was the only proper test in a self-respecting service.

More than that, we were unsympathetic to the whole idea of counting heads by religion. We thought it unworthy, derogatory, irrelevant, retrograde and more and more out-of-date. We were therefore glad to see the anachronistic question about religion in the decennial census returns at long last reduced from a compulsory to an optional question in the 1971 Census; and we felt vindicated when 9.4 per cent chose not to answer the question.

In 1981 no fewer than 22 per cent refused to answer. Knowing the rapidly changing outlook of young people in Ulster today one may expect that figure to keep on rising, making a farce of the foolish idea of highlighting and exacerbating one of the very factors that had bedevilled Irish life in earlier times. Figures about religion in public life all too easily provide small-minded bigots with ammunition for their sordid battles. What matters is citizenship, acceptance of the regime, allegiance, passports and participation in civic affairs. Let religion stay a private and sacred matter.

The Political System

So far this article has spoken of the Administration almost entirely in terms of the departments and the permanent officials. But of course those were merely a part of a wider democratic system with political Ministers in charge. To possibly 90 per cent or so of the people in the Service and of their work Ministers meant little. The doctrine of Ministerial responsibility sometimes disguises the fact that vast amounts of work go on and decisions are taken without the slightest Ministerial intervention or knowledge.

It is only in the senior ranks that officials deal directly with Ministers – for the most part – put proposals to them and get decisions from them. While this is a subtler and much more delicate matter than can be summed up in a sentence or two, it is fair to say that relations with Ministers were good and that the system worked well. Our Ministers were of course less heavily pressed than Ministers in London. But the apocryphal stories one hears of Stormont Ministers leading an idle life of luxury do not fit the facts as most of us know them.[31] Certainly they had nothing like the huge burden of paper work which Whitehall Ministers had to get through; but that may have been no bad thing. Besides, clocking over files in an office all day is not necessarily the sign of an effective Minister. We used to reckon that if he chose to spend as much as half his time outside his headquarters, doing (amongst other things) those two jobs so useful to departments: explaining departmental policies to the public and bringing back public reactions, that was time well spent. Nevertheless in varying degrees and in varying ways Ministers kept in charge and must be given the credit as well as the criticism for all that happened.

The feature which we did not find satisfactory was the presence in departments of junior ministers or Parliamentary Secretaries. They seldom fulfilled any useful function; it was hard to keep them occupied; when Deputations came up they wanted to see the real Minister not the shadow of a Minister. Besides, there were far too many members of the Commons and Senate on the payroll for decency – not that they were paid much or enjoyed many benefits. A leaner political cadre would have served our needs better, we thought.[32]

Much used to be said about the way in which Stormont Ministers kept their activities away from Westminster and about the shameful way in which

Westminster allowed them to do so. Most of it – like most of the criticism –
was superficial and misdirected and told more about the critics than about the
criticised. What was being sought was the right to raise in the Westminster
House of Commons the conduct at Stormont of 'transferred' functions (local
government, housing industry, schooling and so on). In principle this was
wrong. Once you hand over functions to an elected assembly with powers
devolved to it, you cannot then start hashing over what has been done just
because you do not happen to like it. In practice getting good, self-respecting
people to serve on a provincial, devolved assembly is hard enough; to get
them to serve in the knowledge that their debates and decisions were going to
be combed over by another assembly would be impossible. That is common
sense. Thirdly, knowing the determined attitude of Ulster Unionist politicians
one can confidently conclude that any such detailed supervision by another
assembly, far from making them behave differently, would have driven them
further into their 'laager'.

In any case power lay elsewhere. The Home Secretary had a statutory
responsibility. The Home Office was the official channel between Northern
Ireland Government and the British Government. All Acts of the Stormont
Parliament had to receive Royal Assent (and all did, let it always be stressed).
Unionist Ministers were constantly consulting Ministers in Whitehall –
Liberal, Labour, Conservative or coalition. One of the more rational and less
prejudiced criticisms of the Unionist Ministers was in fact that they were too
much in the pockets of Whitehall Ministers and took their line from them far
too readily. When one of our Permanent Secretaries acquired a new Minister
his first job was to chaperone him on a visit to his opposite number in London
(of whatever colour); and after some departmental discussion, tactfully quit
the room and leave the two of them for a confidential chat – presumably about
politics. And did not a prominent Conservative attend each Spring at the
Ulster Unionist Council and give the leading address? Is anyone going to
suggest that in all those ways over all those years British Ministers were not
fully aware of policies and programmes in Ulster? Let us quote Sir Frank
Soskice, Labour Home Secretary in 1965. He had this to say of Ulster
Unionism: 'From England we watch it, we admire it and we rejoice in it'.[33]

At departmental level the same sort of contacts were going on, except that
there were vastly more of them. Our officials kept in close touch with
Whitehall, sometimes for advice and information, sometimes for executive
purposes, as for example at the annual Farm Prices Review. At one time the
Ministry of Commerce acted as a regional office (for certain functions) of the
Board of Trade. All the time there were sensible arrangements for mutual
help: the British Post Office acting as our agent for payment of certain cash
benefits; our Works Branch putting up buildings as agents for the Admiralty.
One weakness was the constant difficulty in getting senior Whitehall officials
to come over and visit us. There ought to have been far more of that (though
Agriculture was again the exception); but they always said they were far too
busy (a weakness in itself). Scottish officials however did visit and were not
afraid to pick our brains on difficult problems, as we did theirs unashamedly.

Politics

Politics were not our business and we took care not to advise Ministers on
political problems. But of course politics impinged on some of our services

and senior officers could not be other than acutely aware. At the price of over-simplifying a notoriously complex affair, let us try to show how the political scene appeared from our subordinate position, and to do so strictly within the spirit and content of this article.

I hope I may presume to speak here for many of my former colleagues for even after all these years I still feel an acute sense of comradeship and loyalty to them.

First, we saw the division in the community as one that was not about religion but about politics, allegiance, acceptance, passport, participation. To some extent this political split coincided – but only to some extent – with the well-known religious split; and religion unfortunately provided all-too-handy if misleading labels.

Second, the political leaders of the nationalists made a blunder by not seeing, by the late 1920s or even by 1945 that the new state had come to stay; that acts of parliament, administrative decisions and benefits were beginning to flow; and that they could serve their people (as well as the Province of which we knew they were proud to be a part) better by placing their aspirations for Irish unity on ice, by throwing in their lot with the state to which they paid their taxes and by muscling in on all that was going on. The negative line which they took led to endless difficulties and frustrations for themselves and their people and was bound to lead them into a whole culture of dissatisfaction and exploitation of grievance; with their knowledge, ability and eloquence they could have done immeasurably better for their people by following a positive line. And we should have enjoyed serving under constitutional nationalists if circumstances had been different.

On the other side the unionists could have tried a lot harder to bring the nationalists in and to offer them a political stake in the future of the Province. They carried the greater responsibility, for they were the majority; they formed the government and held the reins of power; and they had the British government behind them. Theirs seemed to us to be the greater opportunity and therefore the greater shortfall.

Next, in our view neither side could at any serious level be held to be 'blameworthy'. Both were the products of turbulent history and intricate geography. Both were dominated and crippled by constitutional uncertainty, an uncertainty written in to statutes and treaties, prolonged and constantly renewed.[34] It was obvious to us that the constitutional uncertainty led, even incited, the nationalists to look vainly for Irish unity; and it was even more obvious that it repeatedly drove the unionists back into their defensive, intransigent position. Those who created, stimulated and prolonged that constitutional uncertainty have much to answer for in the seemingly endless unrest and violence – the governments of the United Kingdom and the Irish Republic together with those whose advice they chose to take.

Reflections Today

So far this article has tried to present the Administration of 1921–72 as seen by officials at the time. It may help now to look at the Administration from today's standpoint and to see how it appears in this different and perhaps clearer focus.

Many of us recall the sudden invasion in 1968, 1969 and 1970 by journalists, politicians and other investigators who had taken little or no interest in this part of the Kingdom but were suddenly moved to do so by the outbreak of exciting political violence on the streets and by its colourful presentation on television. Most of our visitors at that time, showing no desire to be informed of the facts, went straight to the scenes of disturbances and took their stories from there, in fine disregard of many inconvenient but relevant facts. Those who did come to our offices to be briefed could spare only a few minutes before hurrying on; but in those few minutes revealed – not surprisingly – a terrible ignorance. Off they went, unable to tell the difference between Maghera and Magherafelt, Armagh and Omagh, Kilkeel Urban and Kilkeel Rural, Newry and Newry No. 1 and happily confusing local government electoral affairs with those of Stormont and of Westminster, oblivious of all relevant distinctions between total population and electorate. Legislation, statutory powers, past reforms, practical achievements – all were subordinate to the quest for hot news and instant views on sectarianism, discrimination and so on.

None of us were therefore surprised to see the consequent spate of ill informed and grossly biased material published in Great Britain and abroad. The practical impact of this flood of misrepresentation has had a depressing effect on those of us who had struggled over the years to maintain decent standards and fair administration in a beleaguered situation and in the real world of human endeavour and human imperfection. It is not the job of civil servants to enter into public controversy over such matters. But very few political leaders have spoken out clearly on them. As Arthur Green puts it in opening his article in 'Nationalist Perspectives' and 'Unionist Horizons', *The Review*, Spring 1988: 'Irish Unionists rarely explain themselves. Irish Nationalists seem to do little else.'

Civil Servants are much too modest and much too restrained to take up the cudgels but just occasionally one of our colleagues finds he can thole the persistent calumny no longer and bursts into print, as in this characteristically robust letter to the *Northen Ireland Legal Quarterly* from that great man William Leitch:

CORRESPONDENCE

53 Kensington Road,
Belfast BT5 6NL.

15 December 1981

Dear Sir,

May I, in fairness to myself and my predecessors (the late Sir Arthur Quckett KC LLD and Mr John Foster Caldwell QC LLM), seek the courtesy of your columns to draw your readers' attention to the following questions and answers given in the House of Commons on 3 December 1981:

"5. Mr McCusker asked the Secretary for Northern Ireland if he will list the provisions enacted by the Parliament of Northern Ireland which discriminated between persons or classes of persons on the ground of religious belief.

The Under Secretary of State for Northern Ireland (Mr John Patten): I am not aware of any such provisions.

Mr McCusker: Does the Minister accept that the reference in section 17 of the Northern Ireland Constitution Act 1973 cannot be taken to reflect unfairly on the integrity of those who promoted the legislation under the Government of Ireland Act 1920?

Mr Patten: I am pleased to reassure the hon. Gentleman and the House that section 17 of that Act does not reflect on the competence and, more particularly, the integrity of the draftsmen who drew up that legislation."

This should effectively and finally dispose of the canard that the Parliament of Northern Ireland habitually and unconstitutionally enacted legislation discriminating against persons on the ground of religious belief.

Yours faithfully,

W.A. LEITCH

(formerly First Parliamentary Draftsman to the Government of Northern Ireland).

The Editor,
Northern Ireland Legal Quarterly,
18 University Square,
Belfast 7.

But as Hamlet reminded Ophelia in Act III Scene I:

'be thou chaste as ice, as pure as snow,
thou shalt not escape calumny'

And so we have still had to read since 1972 of Stormont's sectarian housing legislation; of the Protestant University which it set up at Coleraine; of the absence till now of any integrated schools in Ulster; of the concept of One Man One Vote never having been heard of in Ulster; of the distant day when Ulster may eventually reach the stage of that novel concept, trial by jury; of teaching being the only profession open to a young Catholic graduate; of policemen North and South now talking to one another for the first time; and so on and so on. Editors and producers in Great Britain and Eire ought to be ashamed of themselves; and Direct Rule Ministers past and present, could surely do more to nail all those lies. The chagrin felt by superannuated clerks is very real; but it is of no importance compared with the continuing harm done to community relations within Ulster and to the reputation of the Province in the eyes of investors and others outside.

There is much disparaging talk (in somewhat better informed circles) of the way in which reforms had to be pressed on the Stormont Administration by the British Government after 1969 as if the process had started only then and as a response to violence. Looking back, it is hard to see how such statements could be sustained. It was in 1968 that we abolished those two controversial provisions (perfectly honourable but much criticized) the business franchise in local council elections and the University seats at Stormont – off our own bat, as John Whyte neatly puts it. It was in 1967 that we published our pioneering and far-reaching White Paper: *The Re-shaping of Local Government* well ahead of similar reforms in Great Britain and under preparation and consultation since 1965. The Matthew Plan for Physical Development and the Wilson Plan for

Economic Development in the early and mid-1960s represented radical change, the political effects of which were impossible to foresee. The outcome in political terms of our Slum Clearance Act of 1956 was equally hard to foretell. It is easy to say now that these and other changes should have come earlier; but administration, even more than politics, is the art of the possible. We strongly reject the allegation put about since 1972 to the effect that during the 1921–72 period Catholics in Ulster found themselves 'alienated' or were living in 'sullen resentment'. While some political activists may have put themselves in that sort of position, we knew the facts to be very different in practice. We knew for a fact that, whatever their political leanings and aspirations, many leading Catholics were working happily and usefully with Departments every day: councillors, members of statutory boards, members of advisory committees, businessmen, trade unionists, doctors, nurses, lawyers, school managers, head teachers, voluntary workers, farmers and so on. To take just one example from amongst scores: to apply the term 'sullen resentment' to the relations between Newry No. 1 and Newry No. 2 District Councils (both strongly Nationalist) and our Departments would be to stand fact and language on their heads. Those relations were a lot more cordial than relations between some Unionist Councils and Stormont often were. But even those rebuttals do not fully illuminate the heart of the matter. The Northern Ireland Health Service provides volumes of incontrovertible factual evidence concerning the active, intimate and often most distinguished contribution by Catholic Surgeons, Physicians, Scientists, Nurses, Dentists, ambulance drivers and dozens of other categories. The Health Service would have been a great deal poorer without their help; indeed it could hardly have worked. It is that conflict, that dichotomy, between the facts as we knew them and the latter-day political assertions of separation, of 'two alienated communities' that we find distressing and dangerous.

Looking back again over the past 20 years we believe that the tide has begun to turn. Where in the 1970s there was little but denigration of the Administration and constant allegation of earlier oppression and injustice, in the 1980s the facts have started to come out and interpretations to change. One after another, eminent scholars have come forward with painstaking studies of these allegations and have succeeded in reestablishing the truth.

The devastating critique by Professor Christopher Hewitt in the *British Journal of Sociology*, September 1981: 'Catholic Grievance: A Reconsideration', did an immense amount to bring out the truth and to put grievances into perspective. After a severely objective study of facts, figures and, most tellingly, dates, Professor Hewitt concludes: Reforms, far from settling the violence, have not had the slightest effect. Violence has indeed, as everyone knows, got much worse. 'There are two reasons for this: first since the old system was not particularly inequitable, reforms could not have much impact; second the nationalists who predominated in the movement were not really interested in reforms.'

In an even longer article in *Contemporary Irish Studies*, 'How much Discrimination Was There Under the Unionist Regime in 1921–1968?' John Whyte of the Queen's University of Belfast analyses with cool objectivity but with considerable humanity and common sense the old complaints about electoral practice, public employment, private employment and public housing, regional policy and policing and succeeds in putting all these problems into perspective, a perspective that reasonable people of all persuasions would find recognisable and helpful. He speaks of some allegations as being palpably false, others as exaggerated, of truth being obscured by exaggeration and of shades of grey in place of black and white, as previously claimed.

A distinguished graduate of the Queen's University and well-known Belfast man who has devoted much of his life to a meticulous and unrelenting study of these matters – the historian Dr Hugh Shearman gave the world in *The Yearbook of World Affairs 1982* a most trenchant analysis of administration in Ulster and a forthright dismissal of many of the time-worn allegations. He goes far to support Christopher Hewitt in his conclusion that the greater discrimination was exercised by Catholics against Protestants. He includes an open criticism of the Unionist leaders for having failed utterly to speak up for themselves and defend their stewardship and their remarkable achievements.

More encouraging perhaps is the turn of the tide in Great Britain. In his 'Epitaph for a Doomed (Civil Rights) Campaign' in the *Financial Times* on 8 October 1988 John Lloyd leaves the impression that at last the scales are beginning to fall from the eyes of outside commentators, those scales of wishful thinking, of cricketing metaphors, of always siding with the 'underdog' be he right or wrong and the highly political (and doomed) campaign of complaint and denigration. The word he now uses for the present-day outcome of that campaign is 'Hellish'.

It is important that such studies and re-assessments be carried out; it is even more important that they be seen in a positive and constructive light and not as games in an everlasting football league where points are eternally totted up for and against, in the battle against relegation. What mattered to us at the time (and what concerns us still in our restless and anguished retirement) was the carrying on of an administration as good, as liberal and as humane as political conditions allowed. We thought (and we still think) that – when and where political conditions allow – the Ulster community is much less divided than the world has been led to believe; that people from all sections have benefited greatly from and have contributed greatly to a lively, colourful and stimulating public and social life; and that dedicated administration has helped (and can still help) most Ulster people to experience 'the good life' – an approach that would have been understood over two thousand years ago by Plato and Aristotle, in their very different ways.

NOTES

1. The conditions are vividly described and well documented in Brian Barton's work: *The Government of Northern Ireland 1920–1923* (Athol Books, 1980) (M. A. thesis). The most telling original source remains the Speech by Mr R. D. Megaw in introducing the Civil Authorities (Special Powers) Bill on 21 March 1922, columns 86 to 91 of Hansard.

2. For a fuller analysis of the administrative systems and experiences see my autobiography, *Working at Stormont*, published in 1978 by the Dublin Institute of Public Administration .

3. To sum up a most complex situation: The transferred functions were those firmly transferred to Belfast and included education, social services, industry, agriculture, local government, roads, water, police and the lower courts. The reserved functions were, broadly, those temporarily reserved by London and intended for a Council of all Ireland and eventually a united Ireland:- external trade, shipping, radio, posts, coinage, trade marks, patents and much else. As things turned out, they

remained permanently reserved to London. The excepted functions were those wholly retained by the central government in London as a matter of understandable principle: the Crown, the Succession, foreign affairs, treaties, the Armed Forces, passports, visas and immigration. It was in the overlap, shortfall or dubiety of those categories of functions that day-to-day problems arose. A simple example was our power to administer harbours without being able to touch merchant shipping. A more far-reaching difficulty arose out of our duty to protect our cash benefits, public housing, health service, electoral registers and other arrangements (paid for by our taxpayers and ratepayers) from applicants across an open land border but without powers to control immigration or cross-border travel.

4. In one Department we had (a) senior administrators every week (b) joined by professional heads of services every month and (c) augmented by the lawyer, the auditor, the geologist, the chemist and so on once a quarter.

5. Professor J. W. Blake (then at the University College of North Staffordshire) in his official history *Northern Ireland in the Second World War* (London: HMSO, 1956).

6. I am in a position to confirm all of this from personal experience as Hon. Secretary and as Chairman over many years of the Association of Voluntary Grammar Schools, a formidable body in closest touch with its fifty or sixty schools. In a very different idiom the same conclusions are borne out by the Response of the Catholic Colleges to the Chilver proposals on Teacher Training (an undated printed booklet in the mid-1980s).

7. Contained as an Appendix to Constantine Fitzgibbon's work, *Red Hand: The Ulster Colony.*

8. It fell to me in 1983 to act as non-playing captain of an expert group of British health chiefs investigating management and finance at the Royal Victoria Hospital Group on the Falls Road in West Belfast. We did not receive one single complaint about medical or nursing care. Admittedly we were not inviting complaints (as we had more than enough on our hands); but experienced investigators will agree that it must be unusual for a group of five people to spend six months in and around a busy hospital group in such a dangerous urban situation, at formal meetings as well as scores of informal encounters, and not be besieged with complaints. We came away convinced that a high and wholly acceptable level of care was being given to Protestant and Catholic, gunman and victim, bomber and bombed by a devoted and skilled staff at all levels. That was why, in addition to our formal report, we issued an informal leaflet conveying our findings and our appreciation to members of staff far beyond and below the decision-makers.

9. The final decisions on location taken by industrialists were usually on hard-headed grounds of practical advantage to their operations; but not always. Some were swayed by appearances or prejudices, . As for example the prospective Managing Director who after an extensive tour of the West and intensive briefing by our officials turned his head away, kicked a pebble on the tarmac at Aldergrove and muttered: 'I am impressed by everything you have shown me but I am afraid my wife would be happier living near Belfast . . . the shops you know . . .'.

10. *Working at Stormont*, p. 134.

11. Cmd 5460: Oct. 1973, para 1256.

12. One outstanding exception was the support readily given by the nationalists to the Rent Restriction reforms contained in the Housing Act of 1956.

13. I believe that a good Parliamentary system ought to be flexible enough to allow for some such a service in one form or another.

14. I recall the fair-minded Clerk of a republican Council standing in my office and telling us: 'So far as my crowd are concerned I might as well nail a notice on the Town Hall door: no unionist need apply.'

15. My own parents came up from deep country to Belfast in 1905 as total strangers. For over forty years they brought up a family of seven children (not to mention various 'friends' from the homeland) in a succession of five rented houses owned

by commercial landlords. My parents had their many difficulties over rent and repairs, of course, but never once were they heard to complain about their treatment in the matter of housing nor, so far as I know, even to think of applying to the Belfast Corporation.

16. Omagh Rural, for instance.

17. The records of Castlereagh Rural Council will confirm this.

18. I must share the responsibility for this failure for I was one of those in a position to exert a little bit of influence. I confess I thought at the time that the more urgent job was to push on with the new creative and exciting services: Tuberculosis, the Health Service, the new social welfare services, the Housing Trust and so on. Besides, even then I knew instinctively that there were never any thanks to be earned from reforming local government, as I was to confirm in practice 20 years later when we set about reshaping the system in 1965, ahead of Great Britain.

19. H C 2076 of 26 Jan. 1971.

20. In using these statements from the Ombudsman in my autobiography I took the precaution of submitting to Sir Edmund the full typescript of my book for comment, criticism and confirmation. As a result I added this one-line paragraph: 'I am proud to have belonged to such a service', *Working at Stormont*, pp. 238 9.

21. Commonly known as the Crowther-Kilbrandon Commission. Their Report is in Command Paper 5460, Oct. 1973.

22. Op. cit., para 1259 and related passages.

23. Published by Longman, 1980.

24. Rosemary Harris, *Prejudice and Tolerance in Ulster* (Manchester: Manchester University Press, 1972), p. 174.

25. The Chief Establishment Officer of the whole Administration (that is, the chief personnel officer) who admitted me on my first day was a prominent and most personable Catholic, Sam Sloan. I have been told since that he was a convert but I make no comment on that.

26. 'We had gone over to the enemy. We were lost souls', p. 113.

27. Bileen, a young artless Catholic friend of ours from Carrickfergus, blurted out one day in 1955 when she found that I worked at Stormont: 'A good catholic house now, that's what our Priest said last Sunday.'

28. Myself. I had sat the Competition (a marathon indeed) in 1936 and had failed badly. I tried again in 1937 and scraped through. My Catholic friends at Queen's (and companions in many a student encounter) sneered at me for taking such a step, denouncing the Stormont system as unacceptable and unworthy of support. The irony to me was that several of them were smarter fellows than I was, could easily have passed at the first attempt and would have made splendid administrators. Discrimination?

29. Practically unnoticed a charming and most talented girl was promptly welcomed into the powerhouse of the Treasury Division of Ministry of Finance.

30. 'How Much Discrimination was there under the Unionist Regime 1921-1968?' *Contemporary Irish Studies*, p. 12.

31. As it happens, every single Minister I worked close to (from Billy Grant in 1938 to Roy Bradford in 1972) was a hard worker.

32. For a fuller discussion for radical change in these and other related issues, see my 'Ulster Today and Tomorrow', *Political and Economic Planning*, 1978.

33. Quoted by Paul Arthur in *Parliamentary Affairs*, Vol. 30, No. 1 (Winter 1977).

34. My detailed analysis appeared in *The Political Quarterly*, Vol. 59, No.4 (Oct. 1988).

On Visions, Dreams and New Thinking

Recalling Habakkuk, the minor prophet who complained about the iniquity of the wicked being allowed to continue so long, I finished off an Article for the London Policy Studies Institute once with the words: "*Write the vision and make it plain*." It was by no means a high-falutin' piece; it was a rather pedestrian Article devoted to a long series of administrative suggestions for improving the Ulster situation and was entitled: "*Headway in Ulster. Some Practical Ideas.*" Part of my notion in quoting Habakkuk was to prompt Ulster people to call to mind for themselves those other Biblical sayings in favour of thinking big, such as: "*Where there is no vision the people perish*", which they know very well and often used to quote. That Article, with those closing words, was deemed worth re-printing by two very different Publishers, one in London and one in Belfast.

Although any special experience I may have had in various parts of the world is essentially hum-drum, at the dreary edges of administration and politics, I can never escape the reflection that the human spirit needs something bigger if the human situation is to be improved, some grander vision, some voicing of the ideals that people cherish in their hearts even if they do not or can not express them for themselves. In the course, for example, of my tedious book for the famous P.E.P. in 1978 I went out of my way to plead for "*courage and a high note of idealism*".

When, quite separately, after analysing the working of the Stormont Civil Service at great length and with all its shortcomings, in my "*Working At Stormont*" I wrote the one-line paragraph: "*I am proud to have belonged to such a service*" I knew in my bones that I was voicing the unspoken feelings of hundreds of my anguished colleagues. Letters and messages that reached me afterwards bore out the full force of that claim.

Leadership is needed in Ulster to-day. As Professor D.L.Savory used to insist to us at Queen's: "*The Ulster people combine the grit and tenacity of the Scots with the wit and imagination of the Irish.*" While the grit and tenacity are blazingly evident in Ulster public life to-day, the wit and imagination are, shall we say, a little less so.

(Let it not be thought that someone like myself is untroubled by doubts and self-examination over his feelings of national identity. Far from it. I, too, had to search my heart again and again in my earlier years and perhaps I can convey something of the conflict of my position in a frontier society in this way. Prolonged research into family history impressed on me the historical depth, the moral strength and the lasting values of my Ulster-Scot ancestry and upbringing. My pulse-rate tells me I am Irish when I see the green jerseys run out on to the rugby field at Twickenham, or when I hear the haunting strains of the Londonderry Air, or when I am forced to listen in England to ignorant anti-Irish jokes. My reason tells me that I am British in the dimensions of democracy, law and liberty. I am proud to acknowledge all three loyalties and I count myself the richer because of them.)

After so much suffering the people within Ulster need a lift, a brightening of their sky, an injection of hope. It is not that they are in despair but rather in a steadily declining position made up of helplessness and above all futility. "What's the use? What can we do about it all? Who cares about us? Which political party at Westminster cares a fig for our plight?" Many people enduring the endless bombing, the tiresome bomb-hoaxing, the destruction of their jobs, the perpetual inconvenience of road checks and of rings of steel, of having to abandon their transport again and again to walk home in the rain – many a people in that miserable situation would have been complaining to high heaven as well as to Westminster, Brussels, Strasbourg, United Nations and everywhere else. But they don't complain much. That is not the style of the law-abiding, patient people. They display instead an air of stoicism streaked, alas, with helplessness. The whole tragedy, as I tried to argue in an invited Article in the "*Contemporary Review*" in August 1988 (read in sixty-six countries, I was assured) had quite plainly been allowed to drag on too long. In a word, most people have had enough, are fed up and feel let down.

Just as the State cannot make people happy and can do no more than create the conditions in which men and women can lead the good life and reach happiness for themselves, so also is it pointless to ask of Direct Rule Ministers that they should set out to make people cheerful and optimistic. But they have the power to go far to create the conditions in which people will begin to feel hope rising again.

It was most encouraging to see the way in which the Ulster Town Planners launched their 1994 proposals for Belfast City Centre. Rather than produce a plan or a programme they released their ideas as: "*Vision for the Future*", earning at the same time the remarkable tribute from their British President, Hazel McKay: "There's more planning going on here than in the whole of the rest of the United Kingdom." Altogether, the very sort of uplifting approach that is needed and that will benefit us all.

Leadership comes best from known, trusted, local people, people with personality, individuality and colour and that is one of the things most missing in the last twenty years. It is not fully appreciated in Great Britain and abroad how deeply Ulster suffered when local society was decapitated with the abolition of the Stormont Parliament and the dropping of the post of Governor. Whatever their rights and wrongs, whatever their short-comings, whatever each of us may have thought of them individually, those leaders, on all sides, did offer leadership in a recognized and structured setting. And most people liked it, including many in the nationalist minority, as I know.

Some examples stand out as, for instance, when Billy Grant in a memorably bantering speech at the Grand Central Hotel totally eclipsed the visiting English Minister, H.U.Willinck, a most distinguished politician and lawyer. Or when Roy Bradford, at the Culloden, stunned H.E. the solemn German Ambassador with a speech in racy, witty, modern, idiomatic German that was totally impromptu as I have every reason to know. Or when Brian Faulkner, in wellington boots, visited the stricken householders in a flooded Fort Street and ordered on the spot the free laundering of their sodden carpets – off the Falls Road, in West Belfast, where a Republican sniper could easily have picked him off from any upstairs window. Some fifty houses turned out of course to have had many hundreds of downstairs carpets badly in need of laundering. Or when some of us, fearful, timidly approached Gerry Fitt with a suggestion that he might possibly, somehow, see his way to co-operate with his total opposite and alleged enemy Bill Craig, only to be laughed at by the ineffable Gerry: "Why not? What are your afraid of? So long as we are aiming at the same goal!" Or the acute sense of relief – as I have recorded many times – when we sent Austin Currie, the radical nationalist, into some Parliamentary battle or dangerous political encounter, confident that he would acquit himself brilliantly and far surpass any briefing we might have given him. We would have done anything for men like that. Such is the power of leadership.

What is needed now again is leadership in the idiom of to-day and to-morrow. It is certainly not further research that is needed. I have believed for a long time that Ulster must be the most researched community in the world and I have found most of that research pretty useless. It was good to have those impressions substantially borne out by John Whyte in his scholarly and even-handed book: "Interpreting Northern Ireland" summing up and appraising the vast library of research. "There is a case for saying that it has not [been worth while] . . . One might deduce that research actually does harm". I was then amused to read of the anguish with which John Whyte tried to decide whether my Memoirs "should be dignified by the title 'research'." Thank you very much. He need not have bothered his head. If he had spoken to me – and we were friends – I could have put him out of his agony by assuring him that my Memoirs carried no such pretensions. I should have advised him simply to re-print the monosyllabic words with which that book opens: "I wish to tell how I tried to do my job and earn my pay during forty years in the Northern Ireland Civil Service". Hardly a recipe for pretentious research, was it?

I prefer action.

By 1990 I was so intensely worried by the whole Ulster problem, internal and external, and foresaw so much frustration ahead that I decided to approach individually every Member of the House of Commons and the House of Lords whom I knew personally or with whom I had had any working association over the years. Wishing to spare them the embarrassment of talking about seeing visions or dreaming dreams I spoke instead of the need for new thinking. In the end I wrote long letters to no fewer than fifty Members, sketching a whole catalogue of new ideas and crying out for new thinking by all concerned. The responses, in various forms, were courteous, friendly, appreciative, even painstaking but not, alas, reflecting any great inclination to face new thinking.

Who, then, might give a lead in new thinking? While it is mainly for the Ulster people themselves to make the effort there are some outstanding exceptions. The I.R.A. war, I insist, is with Britain and is basically Britain's problem to solve. Relations with the Irish Republic are also basically for Britain, the sovereign international power, not for Ulster a subordinate province with no standing in international affairs. But within the local community, under Government and in concert with Government, the people have much to do; and it is right to say they have tried to do much already. But the experience of many well-meaning local initiatives since 1972 has shown that they fall far short of what they might achieve and that they can do little without support, without structures and without some measure of sustained public leadership. Without those, they have been little more than passing gestures, flickers of goodwill in a darkening world.

Why not set up a new office of First Citizen, consisting of a triumvirate of two men and one woman performing ceremonial jobs from Hillsborough and setting standards of decency, honour and impartiality?

Why not have an up-to-date Privy Council of, say, five men and four women, to examine, to consult and to advise on major new proposals? Meeting alternately in Derry, Enniskillen, Newry, Coleraine and Bangor?

Why not have in each Direct Rule team one Minister drawn by arrangement from Her Majesty's Opposition at Westminster to set an example and show how coalition and power-sharing (surprisingly demanded of Ulster in her vastly more difficult conditions) can be made to work by sensible people?

Why not have a Joint Local Assembly indirectly elected by all the District Councils to give voice to current local feelings and demands?

Why not gradually build in to each Direct Rule team of Ministers one non-party local man or woman who has proved himself or herself in public life (if need be, elevated to the House of Lords) until in a few years the whole team is Ulster-based, working under the authority of H.M.Government of the day? The present rigid colonial system of Ministers flying in and out is not only belittling but wildly out-of-date, reminiscent of the last days of the French in Algiers, a long time ago now, I seem to remember.

Why not make a start on creating a Senate without party affiliations? As I argued at length in my PEP book in 1978 there can be few countries more in need of a non-party upper chamber than Ulster – a forum for Quakers, Jews, the main churches, farmers, youth, trade unions and professional associations, industry, social work, the arts, pop music, sport, yes even motor-cycling and boxing, to express the views of concerned people until Talks about Talks can produce the real forum for democratic politics.

Why not ask the Churches, so active and so co-operative in Ulster, to increase hugely their part in positive moral leadership, preaching seven days a week the difference between good and evil, between right and wrong in the harsh world of present-day reality, stressing the message of love, mercy, compassion and forgiveness throughout their communities, to the violent men and women in the pubs and the clubs rather than just to the faithful in the pews? Could they perhaps make a start by advising their people to reduce their drinking by seventy-five per cent, to put their money into Ulster Savings Certificates and to rebuild the Ulster ethic of hard work and saving for a rainy day?

Why not take time by the forelock and set up the strongest defences now against the flood of drugs and inner city crime that is likely to sneak in from England and Scotland to fill the place of terrorism when that eventually ends?

What aims might we set ourselves in the field of public and political affairs? What hopes do we dream of? What vision of Ulster do we wish to put before the people? What new thinking is needed?

To get rid of the IRA within a year by more intensive Police work, by hiring the best brains in Britain, by withdrawing the Army to barracks only to come out sternly when called, and by having talks at all levels with IRA and Sinn Fein. To renounce the corrosive doctrine of Reginald Maudling about 'an acceptable level of violence'. To banish religion from political life and terrorist reporting. To promote far more jobs in areas ravaged by the IRA. To eschew every public policy, however well meaning, that has the effect of splitting the community. To abandon the lamentable Anglo-Irish Agreement and to use instead the existing British-Irish Joint Parliamentary Body, making it work a lot harder than it has ever done. To press for the dropping of Articles 2 and 3 from the Eire Constitution. To promote every measure that promises to bind the community together, building on the unity and cohesion of all those many examples of success that everyone knows already exist – such as the Courts of Law, the Universities, the Hospitals, the Ambulance crews, the arts, the statutory boards, the Housing Executive, the Civil Service and so on; and building also on the traditionally low level of non-terrorist violence in this extraordinary province. To shun any political party that does not fully support the Police and encourage its young men and women to join. To expose blarney and to reject casuistry. To break down the bigger Secondary Schools or High Schools into smaller Workshops, Laboratories, Studios, Model Farms, Nurseries, Bureaux with their own names and flags so as to get away from the jejune split between Grammar Schools and the rest and to encourage the new units to surpass the Grammar Schools in the urge to do well, in pride, in civic duty and in popular acclaim. To set some ambitious goals in social and environmental affairs to which every citizen can contribute and from which every citizen can benefit. To get away from having a 'permanent majority and a permanent minority' in politics by calling for new parties. To guarantee every citizen his or her civil rights, with the strictest laws, firmly linked in every case to corresponding duties and obligations. To bring back to public and political life all those who have abandoned the public stage and harness their abilities, energies and imagination. And of course in every field, to have friendly co-operation with the Republic (on a voluntary and informal footing wherever possible because that is where the Irish, North and South, are at their best). To build again an Ulster that is peaceful and peaceable, well run, hard working, outward looking, enjoying two contrasting cultures, an Ulster of which we can all be so proud that we feel uplifted when people say to us: "So you're from Ulster, are you? You've been through the fire all right. You have done some very foolish things but at any rate your metal has been assayed once again!"

Having sketched those obvious aims I am aware that it is now a long time since I last held any official position or elective office from which I might be able to act. It is for younger men and women in public positions to-day to think about those aims – and any other aims – to approve, reject, amend or add to them and then to promote the leadership that will bring new hope and confidence. I have no doubt that they will improve on every suggestion I have made for I am ever conscious of my limitations. My stance is one of opening up a problem, of turning it round to look at it from many different points of view and then of putting up suggestions; not of issuing pronouncements, not by any means. After all, who am I to pronounce? What do I know? I come back again and again to the great Essayist, Montaigne, who philosophically asked himself, exactly as I do:

"Que sais-je?"